# LEADS TO RESULTS

# TABLE OF CONTENTS

# About the Authors

Richard Bufkin
**President**
Senior Direct, Inc. / Target Leads

I grew up in Dallas and have a sister and two brothers. I graduated from Jesuit High School and those formative years with the Jesuits taught me to put others before myself, to be a "Man for Others." I am proud of this mindset and try to live it every day.

I went to Colorado College, a small liberal arts college where I majored in Religion and played lacrosse.

After college, I lived and traveled through South America then moved to San Francisco two months before the Dot Com Bust!

With all of the tech dollars drying up faster than water on a sidewalk during a Dallas summer, I did something very smart and unexpected. I went to work as a paralegal. I thought that, just maybe, I wanted to be an attorney.

However, before I committed my life to law school, debt and a lifetime of practicing law, I knew that I needed a much better understanding of what the day-to-day life of an attorney really meant.

No disrespect to attorneys, I have two of them in my family, I quickly discovered that this was not for me.

After my committed year of employment and unparalleled education into litigation, I was asked to give the family business a try.

Again, I committed to a one year trial.

Quickly, I discovered this was for me.

I love creating marketing programs, I love to build things (like TL LeadManager), and I love to see people and companies succeed.

I am deeply committed to our success and I am equally committed to yours. Without your success, ours becomes impossible.

*Richard Bufkin*

## Lloyd Lofton L.U.T.C.
## **<u>Managing Partner</u>**
## 7 Figure Sales Tools

I was selling Amway products at the age of 16, eventually becoming a Direct Distributor. I sold swimming pools when I turned 18 and for a while ran my own painting company, at age 19 in Garden Grove, California.

My partner and I had some business cards made, parked our car in a neighborhood, he on one side of the street, me on the other and we went door-to-door selling trim touch ups for $95.00 (in 1972), one story, one color house paint for $295 and we were off. I think that first week we got three jobs. All of a sudden, we had a business.

I started selling insurance in 1977 with John Hancock, as a debit agent (which most people have no idea what that is now) in Alton, Illinois. I sold the first IRA back then in our region and won the top TSA (a retirement plan for non-profits) seller in our region.

I left them in 1979 as a Sales Manager and went across the bridge to Saint Louis, Mo where I was an agent with Combined Insurance Company. They kept us in a hotel for two weeks, no break, learning a primary sales script and three ancillary tag-on sales scripts, word-for-word, along with three standard rebuttals before we could be released to sell in the field. I became a field trainer for them, taking new sales people down the street in residential and business districts selling policies door-to-door, eventually becoming a regional trainer. Since then I have run my own agency, served as a Director for a carrier captive sales distribution, ran a call center, built a credit card processing and small business finance distribution and written articles for several industry related magazines.

I have been interviewed by The Wealth Channel through American College, been an instructor of college courses in sales and management through Chattahoochee Technical College, host training's through Lorman Education and served as a Vistage speaker.

I know you will receive no better lead training than in this book. I understand how all the different parts fit together, from your business plan, activity plan, approach, scripts, presentation, closing to listening and asking questions.

Some of you will say "I used to do this" or "I had a manager who used to teach this" to those who never heard of some of the techniques you will learn here and you will find amazing results.

Here's my best advice, go through this book, find your selling style, make as many mistakes as you can, as fast as you can to shorten the learning curve.

You are the next thing you do so make it **BIG**....and make it **MATTER!**
Remember, if you want to make more.........**GET BETTER!**

# Lloyd Lofton L.U.T.C.

## INTRODUCTION

The goal of this book is to ensure you have a good understanding of how prospecting tools will enable you to be successful in developing an activity plan to ensure a full day of sales activity.

Through a variety of prospecting channels, including a number of direct mail pieces, telemarketer leads, profiled lists and customer referrals, this book demonstrates the opportunity to contact your target market.  It is then up to you to meet the needs of these prospects with the most appropriate products in your portfolio.

One advantage of this book is that it illustrates how salespeople can have an entire day's worth of sales activity in a workable geographic area.  By clustering Hot Leads, Anniversary Leads, Orphan Leads, Profile Leads, Turning 65 Cards, Turning 66-69 Cards and Turning 70 cards by zip code, and matching the zip code to that of your Direct Mail responses, telemarketed leads, referral leads, company provided leads, Take One Leads or Seminar Leads, it's possible to compile an entire day's activity in a few zip codes.  You spend more of your day contacting prospects and less traveling through your territory.

After reading this book, you will have a system to manage and utilize your lead database. The book focuses on helping you with the skill sets to get the best return out of your investment in your lead programs. This includes ordering, tracking, approaching and overcoming objections from prospects who have indicated an interest in your products or services.

We start off with helping you calculate your goals and develop an activity plan. Then we go into detail of the different lead sources available, illustrated through a Wheel of Fortune format. Next, we show you how to manage your time and keep an activity tracking form to ensure you measure the things you need to do the most to reach your goal. Then we review how to approach these prospects, providing scripts, and rebuttals to objections.

You will get an in-depth review of multiple lead types leading to tips on utilizing scripts while then having a variety of scripts presented. Within this section, you will have the opportunity to learn some standard rebuttals to the four basic objections you will receive from prospects.

Lastly you will be taken through all the lead types you can order, their intended purpose, how to work, why to approach and each having a specific script to use in your call to schedule an appointment.

This will be the most complete and comprehensive book on leads you can get.

With determination, effort and follow-thru you will build a seven-figure business and a six-figure income.

## Selling is your game...NOW IS YOUR TIME TO WIN!

# CHAPTER 1 - CALCUTE GOALS AND ACTIVITY

Take your annual goal amount and divide it by the number of weeks you expect to work this year.

Example: 2 weeks of vacation leaves me with 50 work weeks, minus two weeks for the holiday seasons, and illnesses, leaving 48 weeks.

$80,000.00 / 48 weeks = $1667.00 needed to earn each work week.

At an estimated $540 in commission per sale, 3.5 sales weekly are needed to reach this goal.

You will close one out of every three appointments you actually go on, as a new salesperson. This means 10 booked appointments are needed to make 3.5 sales.

On average, you can count on a third of your booked appointments canceling, so for 10 appointments to actually run, you will need to book 15 appointments.

One hour of marketing should yield one appointment on the telephone or three appointments in face-to-face visits. So, on average, you will need to spend 15 hours a week marketing to meet this goal of $80,000.00 income a year.

Each appointment will average one and one-half hours and one hour round trip travel time.

15 hours of marketing
25 hours appointment running and travel time
5 hours of paperwork and administrative follow up
5 hours of "waste and miscellaneous"
5 hours of education and meetings / personal study
Total average workweek for this goal is 55 hours

## MY GOAL FOR 20__ BUSINESS YEAR IS:

|  | Annual Income Goal |  | Annual Business Mix |  |
|---|---|---|---|---|
| 1. | 1st Year Commission | $ _____ | Major Medical | _____ % |
| 2. | Number of weeks I will work | _____ | Ancillary Product | _____ % |
| 3. | Divide 1 by 2 = Total $ weekly | _____ | Medicare Supplement | _____ % |
| 4. | 1st Year Commission per sale | _____ | Ancillary Product | _____ % |
| 5. | Divide 4 into 3 = Sales per week | _____ | Life | _____ % |
| 6. | Gross written business | _____ | LTC | _____ % |
| 7. | Taken Rate | _____ | Term | _____ % |
| 8. | Divide 7 into 6 = Net issued | _____ | Annuity | _____ % |

- Tailor your business plan to meet this hourly goal, for example, make sure you have 15 hours of marketing shown and accounted for, etc.
- Don't let your number of hours decrease. Fill in extra time with more appointments and more marketing. 'Kicking back' in my first year is very tempting, but a very bad idea, and will work against accomplishing your goals.

**Keys to Successful Prospecting**

Prospecting support provided to you by your manager or company will, in most cases, account for approximately 30% of your business while the other 70% will come from your own prospecting activities.

To maximize your productivity, keep these points in mind:
- Follow a telephone script that works for you. Once you find what works for you, don't "fix" it; stick with what works for you.
- Only sell the appointment, do not get caught in the trap of answering product or price questions on the phone.
- Ask for introductions from everyone you talk to, even if you don't make a sale.
- Win the community markets where you work.
    - √ Go to the house or business on each side and across the street of your appointment
    - √ Leave your information with each house or business that you visit
    - √ Collect business cards from each business you visit
- Use "I'm not interested" and "I already have [insert your product/service here]" responses as stop by meet and greet time between appointments. "I'm not interested" may mean that they did not have time, and "I already have [insert your product/service here]" may mean they are just used to what they have. Continue to follow up with these prospects.
- When you call telemarketer activity, make sure you are speaking with the same person as the telemarketer did. For internet activity, make sure it is the person who completed the request.

**Wheel of Fortune**

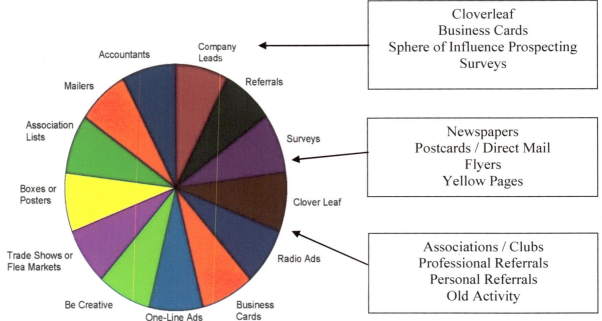

- Cloverleaf: Introduce yourself to three or four businesses located geographically close to a prospect or appointment. Before seeing prospect A, go next door and say that you are on your way to see [prospect's name] and that you would like to stop by afterwards. Introduce yourself and ask preliminary questions.
- Business Cards: Collect business cards from everyone that you meet. Collect the business cards from restaurants that have giveaways. Set out "fish bowls" for a free lunch to collect cards.
- Sphere of Influence Prospecting: Prospect where you pay, where you play, and where you pray.
- Surveys: Conduct surveys at shopping plazas or malls.
- Newspapers: Small print ads, "one-liners" or reader ads in classified sections of local papers, shoppers, and programs.
- Postcards/Direct Mail: Obtain voter, club, church lists; purchase small business lists or profiled names. Use approved direct mail if your product/company require.
- Flyers: Post flyers on bulletin boards, leave them in doors when people are not home, insert them in local newspapers, or arrange to hand them out at sporting events.
- Yellow Pages: Yellow Page books are a great resource to identify small business owners. Pick up a book or use Yellowpages.com and start calling or utilize the cloverleaf tactic.
- Associations / Clubs: Join the chamber of commerce, obtain lists from local trade groups such as homebuilders, or join clubs such as Rotary.
- Professional Referrals: partner with accountants, P&C agents, financial planners…to obtain referrals for health insurance.
- Personal Referrals: Make sure to call existing clients back for referrals and cross sell.
- Old Leads: File your old leads that did not buy according to their insurance company. When that company has a rate increase, call the prospects that turned you down before.

# Weekly Schedule

One key to setting appointments is to always book your appointments from the end of the week to the first of the week. Book Thursday first then work backwards to Tuesday. This ensures you have a full week and removes the false sense of security that occurs when you have several appointments the first part of the week. Also, book your appointments from the end of the day to the beginning of the day to ensure you have a full day.

Monday
- Organize your activity and schedule your appointments for the week starting with Thursday and working backwards.
- Call to set appointments one to one and one-half hours apart to lessen driving time.
- Don't stop calling for appointments until your entire week is full.

Tuesday
- Continue to schedule appointments in the morning if your week is not full.
- Run the appointments you have scheduled.
- Meet decision makers, exchanging business cards, between appointments

Wednesday
- Run the appointments you have scheduled.
- Meet decision makers, exchanging business cards, between appointments

Thursday
- Run the appointments you have scheduled.
- Meet decision makers, exchanging business cards, between appointments

Friday
- Run the appointments you have scheduled.
- Prepare your paperwork for Monday turn-in.
- Self-marketing

**Weekly Tracking**

| Method | Type | Contacts | Appointment Potential | Sales Potential | Annual Volume Potential |
|---|---|---|---|---|---|
| 1. Leads (A & B) | • Phone Contact <br> • Drop Ins | | | | |
| 2. Client/ Prospect Referrals | • After a "Sale" or "No Sale" <br> • Cloverleaf <br> • Unsolicited | | | | |
| 3. Reference Centers | • Accountants <br> • P & C sales people <br> • Financial Planners | | | | |
| 4. Trade show/flea market | • Flea market <br> • B to B expo <br> • Trade show (recruiting/sales | | | | |
| 5. Self-Promotion Self-Marketing | • Newspaper <br> • Take one <br> • Reply cards mailer <br> • Pre-approach letters | | | | |
| 6. Walk – N – Talk | • Office building <br> • Strip mall <br> • Three-foot rule | | | | |
| 7. EDUCATION | • Tapes <br> • Books <br> • Seminars <br> • Company trainings | | | | |
| TOTAL | | | | | |

You will be able to maximize your efforts with your leads and your production *if* you do the following:

- Follow the "telephone appointment script" module. Sell only the appointment—

  (Go to {before we hang up...}) to pre-qualify.

- Get referrals from each person you see or talk to, even if you do not make the sale.

- Work the "golden triangle," which is the two businesses on each side of the business you are calling on, as well as one across the street. Use the "business card approach script."

- Make sure you drop in and see all "I'm not interested" leads. Do not throw them away. A response of "I'm not interested" usually means, "I'm busy right now." Consider that they may have had people lined up at their cash register when you called.

- Make sure you're talking to the same person the telemarketer talked to. If they talked to the wife, that's who you need to be talking to. If they spoke to the husband, you need to be speaking with him.

- Do not try to sell over the phone, for first contact. Set the appointment only. Save the rest for the presentation.

- When you start the appointment, use the "sales presentation script" found in that module.

- A key point to remember is that the salesperson who *asks* for referrals *gets* referrals! Ask for referrals even if you don't make the sale.

## STP! – SEE THE PEOPLE ... STUFF THE POCKETS

- Direct Mail = 1.03% Response average
- Direct Phone Contact = 25% Response
- Face to Face = 50% Response

*TIPS:* 1. Call all your leads at least once every six months
2. Set appointments with the "Hot Prospects"
3. Get in the field and go see everyone else ... even the "not interested" or hang-ups

**Daily Phone Activity Log (example)**

**CONTACTS**:

| 1 | 11 | 21 | 31 | 41 | 51 | 61 | 71 | 81 | 91 |
|---|----|----|----|----|----|----|----|----|-----|
| 2 | 12 | 22 | 32 | 42 | 52 | 62 | 72 | 82 | 92 |
| 3 | 13 | 23 | 33 | 43 | 53 | 63 | 73 | 83 | 93 |
| 4 | 14 | 24 | 34 | 44 | 54 | 64 | 74 | 84 | 94 |
| 5 | 15 | 25 | 35 | 45 | 55 | 65 | 75 | 85 | 95 |
| 6 | 16 | 26 | 36 | 46 | 56 | 66 | 76 | 86 | 96 |
| 7 | 17 | 27 | 37 | 47 | 57 | 67 | 77 | 87 | 97 |
| 8 | 18 | 28 | 38 | 48 | 58 | 68 | 78 | 88 | 98 |
| 9 | 19 | 29 | 39 | 49 | 59 | 69 | 79 | 89 | 99 |
| 10 | 20 | 30 | 40 | 50 | 60 | 70 | 80 | 90 | 100 |

**APPOINTMENTS**:

| | Prospect Name | Telephone | Address |
|---|---|---|---|
| 1 | | | |
| Comments | | | |
| 2 | | | |
| Comments | | | |
| 3 | | | |
| Comments | | | |
| 4 | | | |
| Comments | | | |
| 5 | | | |
| Comments | | | |
| 6 | | | |
| Comments | | | |
| 7 | | | |
| Comments | | | |
| 8 | | | |
| Comments | | | |
| 9 | | | |
| Comments | | | |
| | | | |

# CHAPTER 2 - LEAD TYPES AND MANAGEMENT

## How Real is That Lead?

Love 'em or hate 'em, companies that connect Internet consumers with Sales Professionals are now a part of your business reality. Whether their business model is selling leads or providing a conduit for Sales Professionals to pitch their product/services to consumers, these companies have leveraged the power of the Internet to create new forms of insurance marketing. Typically, these companies obtain consumer leads through some combination of advertising and buying high placements in search engines.

How you feel about Internet lead generation will depend a lot on your own strategies for finding new customers and your comfort level with technology. Some Sales Professionals see Internet leads as the next big thing; others voice opposition to what they see as the appropriation of their hard-won customers.

## The lead is the thing.

For Sales Professionals who have tried and rejected Internet referrals, there's no doubt that the most critical issue is the quality of the leads. Screening out buyers who aren't serious is the biggest challenge for any Internet lead company. Even with screening, does that mean that everyone is a real buyer? No, it doesn't. No more than all the traffic walking into an open store does, nor all the people who walk onto a car lot are buyers.

Most Internet companies make some efforts to screen their leads. Many companies use "proprietary filtering software" to root out unqualified Internet customers. Many use a combination of filtering software and manual verifications of phone numbers to screen its leads.

It is important to understand consumer behavior. First, not everyone is comfortable either using the Internet or typing on the keyboard. Some people tend to do what is comfortable for them. If they are not good at typing numbers, they will not do the address or do just the name of the street. For others, say seniors, they may accidentally hit the NUM LOCK key on the keyboard and the last three numbers of their phone number will not show up.

Any number of incidents can and does happen when people are using the Internet and their keyboard. What does not change is that when they search out information about insurance on the Internet, they click a page that indicates someone will contact them. The fact that Internet buyers visit multiple sites in their searches (an average of 4.17) has caused some Sales Professionals some concern.

"I've bought a lead, then instantly recognized the name as someone who had just bought a policy with a Salesperson I know," some salespeople have stated. Others have commented, "I've also received the same lead from more than one company." But if there's one consistent factor among Sales Professionals who've tried Internet leads is that there is no consistent factor.

You will need to verify the information is current at the time the consumer entered the information on the request page of the vendor's site. Remember, consumer information is dependent on the accuracy of the consumer's typing skills, interest in providing the information and comfort level with the computer

Use additional Internet sources to verify or search information regarding Internet Leads receive such as:

A.  411.com

B.  Mapquest.com

C.  Yellowpages.com

D.  Go to the address and knock on the door

When you call make sure you find out who completed the on-line form, it may not be the person whose name appears on the form. Keep in mind many vendors sell these internet leads as "shared" leads, that is they sell them to up to five salespeople, so the consumer may have already been contacted more than once. If they say they have been contacted already don't act surprised, rather indicate the way these request are processed by the member website is to share with up to five professionals, each with a different offering, product or price and your job is to help them get information for the best offering, product or price and to do so you have to ask a couple of questions.

Remember questions "gather" information, objections "disclose" information.

## Consumer Lists

Names are emailed to you starting as little as five cents per name!

Consumer lists are great prospecting tools for your own telemarketing or mailing programs. Narrow your prospect pool by a number of demographics including exact age, estimated household income and more.

Vendor consumer database is made up of over 240 million consumers and can be segmented by numerous demographics so you can reach just the right prospective customer with your specific message. Whether you are looking for exact age, selections by income or net worth, ethnicity, homeowners, or numerous other selects...these and more lists are available.

Lists are processed through USPS standards giving you the most complete addresses, and is 100% ZIP+$© coded. In addition, all list orders are processed through DPV to ensure accurate mail delivery. The file is compiled at the individual level allowing you to target the right person in the household by name.

Hundreds of sources are used to compile the list including public records, phone directories, U.S. Census data, consumer surveys and purchase transactions, as well as other proprietary sources. The result is a rich and accurate data source to drive your marketing efforts.

## Email Format

This is the most popular way for consumers to receive their prospecting lists. Email lists can be sent in Excel, ASCII, or D-Base formats.

When you receive your list via email, it is easy for you to import into your current contact management system or have directly deposited into your TL LeadManager® system, create mail merge letters and/or mail merge labels, print your own call list, etc.

You also don't have to wait for the list to be shipped to you so turn time is much faster.

| State | EMail | Fname | Lname | Address | County | City | Zip | Phone Number | Gen | DOB | IncomePe | AverageHo | Source | IP | Date and Time |
|---|---|---|---|---|---|---|---|---|---|---|---|---|---|---|---|
| FL | ange...71@...cc | Crystal | Stubblefield | 549 | DUVAL | Jacksonville | 32258 | 9045714127 | F | 7/27/1971 | $70,131 | $124,900 | www.123freetr | 68.218.1 | 3/24/2010 1:44 |
| FL | ang... | Kaylyn | Mann | 279 | PASCO | Wesley chapel | 33544 | 8134827161 | M | 4/9/1968 | $53,427 | $121,000 | www.myamazir | 70.126.1 | 3/28/2010 5:07 |
| FL | ANGEL... | ANGELA | JORDAN | 76 | nc ORANGE | ORLANDO | 32810 | 4072194038 | F | 2/5/1974 | $39,185 | $88,600 | zippayday.com | 72.92.11 | 2/17/2010 7:48 |
| FL | ange...et | Angela | Wilson | 130 | HILLSBOROUGH | Tampa | 33612 | 8139336814 | F | 1/2/1970 | $26,985 | $74,300 | www.123freetr | 72.91.94 | 3/25/2010 23:10 |
| FL | ange...yahoo.c | Angela | Romero | 1807 | MIAMI-DADE | Miami | 33135 | 3053005681 | F | 7/29/1953 | $18,903 | $126,300 | www.123freetr | 98.64.17 | 3/15/2010 1:38 |
| FL | ange...yahoo.c | ennis | Burkett | 31 ne | ALACHUA | Gainesville | 32641 | 3524679372 | F | 3/26/1963 | $24,903 | $53,000 | regencycashlo | 72.32.30 | 3/30/2010 8:19 |
| FL | ange...net | Angela | Barnes | 680 | rd DUVAL | Jacksonville | 32208 | 9045510583 | F | 12/23/1966 | $31,849 | $58,200 | popularliving.c | 192.245 | 3/30/2010 4:45 |
| FL | ange...com | william | santiago | 205 | d LAKE | groveland | 34736 | 3525574227 | F | 1/1/1966 | $39,368 | $93,700 | www.popularli | 70.121.1 | 4/3/2010 4:38 |
| FL | ange...mai | Angela | Haskins | 181 | circl HILLSBOROUGH | Ruskin | 33570 | 8132447350 | F | 9/14/1961 | $28,822 | $81,300 | classicvacatioi | 199.211 | 3/30/2010 9:40 |
| FL | ange...om | Angela | Price | 1803 | rd DUVAL | Jacksonville | 32225 | 9046106481 | F | 2/12/1951 | $55,966 | $113,300 | netflix.com | 192.157 | 3/27/2010 18:31 |
| FL | ange...om | Angela | Long | 327 | DUVAL | Jacksonville | 32226 | 9047516353 | F | 8/9/1966 | $53,008 | $128,100 | http://www.wa: | 162.77.2 | 3/26/2010 21:29 |
| FL | ange... | Angela | Dickenson | 75 | CLAY | Keystone Heights | 32656 | 3524730197 | F | 6/22/1960 | $39,748 | $89,600 | www.123freetr | 70.152.3 | 3/24/2010 12:40 |
| FL | ange...cor | Angela | Jones | 11 | a: VOLUSIA | Deland | 32720 | 3864905196 | F | 7/27/1963 | $32,688 | $81,200 | popularliving.c | 192.108 | 4/2/2010 16:05 |
| FL | angel...mai | Angel | Sanchez | 41 | MARION | Ocala | 34476 | 3522916956 | F | 2/2/1985 | $35,738 | $97,500 | www.123freetr | 76.3.30. | 3/28/2010 6:13 |
| FL | angel...om | Csa | Bau | 39 | ce LEE | Cape coral | 33909 | 2394588356 | M | 4/26/1968 | $42,541 | $83,700 | betheboss.com | 198.137 | 3/27/2010 21:32 |
| FL | angel...cor | Angel | Limery | 107 | le ORANGE | Orlando | 32836 | 4073348740 | F | 3/10/1955 | $77,273 | $243,100 | www.netdebt.cc | 192.131 | 03/30/2010 05:10:00 |
| FL | angel...ho.co | Amy | Lester | 142 | ircl HILLSBOROUGH | Odessa | 33556 | 8137498002 | F | 9/22/1956 | $71,141 | $187,200 | www.debtshiek | 209.93.7 | 03/30/2010 05:04:00 |
| FL | angel...yah | Junice | Adame | 50 | et COLLIER | Immokalee | 34142 | 2393770577 | F | 10/19/1972 | $25,189 | $67,100 | www.123freetr | 64.37.68 | 3/16/2010 4:27 |
| FL | angel...com | Angel | Beauchamp | 156 | ou MARION | Ocala | 34473 | 3525536847 | F | 12/24/1959 | $32,523 | $72,700 | 123freetravel.c | 209.8.23 | 3/29/2010 0:25 |
| FL | angel...com | Alexandri | Simmon | 133 | rd DUVAL | Jacksonville | 32225 | 5135202187 | F | 1/28/1971 | $55,966 | $113,300 | www.123freetr | 68.154.1 | 3/12/2010 5:59 |
| FL | angel...com | Angel | Pugh | 528 | dr DUVAL | Jacksonville | 32258 | 9047049811 | F | 12/25/1977 | $70,131 | $124,900 | work-at-home< | 192.138 | 3/27/2010 0:36 |
| FL | angel...ii.c | Angel | Pagan | 110 | ORANGE | Orlando | 32809 | 4072833810 | F | 4/18/1943 | $34,385 | $84,500 | netflix.com | 147.53.1 | 3/27/2010 19:14 |
| FL | ange...ic.co | Louise | Irving | 343 | BROWARD | Miramar | 33023 | 9549834784 | F | 4/21/1956 | $37,756 | $92,400 | getyourprize | 67.191.7 | 3/1/2010 13:29 |
| FL | angca... | Angela | Wheeler | 34 | loop PASCO | New port richey | 34655 | 7273262150 | F | 8/18/1977 | $41,485 | $114,600 | www.123freetr | 71.180.1 | 3/13/2010 5:07 |
| FL | angbra... | angelic | Whelpley-b | 231 | thwes POLK | winter haven | 33880 | 8632937538 | F | 9/7/1957 | $34,293 | $69,200 | www.popularli | 71.101.5 | 4/3/2010 5:57 |
| FL | anfusa... | alvaro | pereira | 848 | ph MIAMI-DADE | miami | 33131 | 3055771011 | m | 7/24/1964 | $56,297 | $223,700 | betheboss.com | 192.190 | 4/4/2010 11:08 |
| FL | anfu...om | bob | sinclair | 45 | MARTIN | stuart | 34997 | 419-419-8780 | m | 3/14/1987 | $42,973 | $143,100 | www.123freetr | 69.163.2 | 4/5/2010 21:20 |
| FL | anec...cor | Ashley | Neconie | 170 | MIAMI-DADE | Miami | 33181 | 7867971767 | F | 12/13/1970 | $32,223 | $211,000 | www.123freetr | 74.175.6 | 3/24/2010 2:13 |
| FL | andy...cor | Anderson | Oliva | 224 | a: PALM BEACH | Boca raton | 33428 | 5616742893 | m | May 6 1978 | $52,266 | $149,400 | studentsreview | 17.190.7 | 3/30/2010 7:30 |
| FL | andy...net | Andrew | Hogan | 2612 | apt BROWARD | Hollywood | 33020 | 9542455354 | F | 10/6/1965 | $28,610 | $92,300 | www.popularli | 98.203.6 | 3/30/2010 13:15 |
| FL | andy...com | andrew | taub | 6046 | circl PALM BEACH | boynton beach | 33487 | 5613641867 | F | 3/11/1972 | $52,531 | $160,300 | www.myamazir | 74.233.1 | 4/3/2010 13:00 |
| FL | andy_m... | Laura | montgomer | 6137 | lot POLK | lake wales | 33898 | 8638525065 | F | 9/23/1961 | $30,802 | $68,500 | tagged | http://w | 4/3/2010 5:02 |
| FL | andy_crash... | Andre | Clarke | 45 Sa | MARION | Ocala | 34472 | 3526872869 | F | 8/15/1972 | $31,726 | $73,900 | studentsreview | 67.232.6 | 4/3/2010 10:00 |

**Peel and Stick Labels**

These (also called Pressure Sensitive Labels) can be used for a number of things. Most clients use them when mailing their own mailers. They just peel the label with the preprinted prospect name and address and affix it to their mailer. Some clients also use them to put on 3 x 5 cards so they can easily keep notes on the prospects after calling on them, something you don't have to do with the TL LeadManager® Standard format is in sheets three-up for a total of 30 to a page. Custom label formats should also be available upon request.

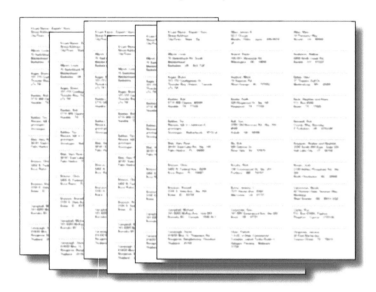

**Manuscript**

This format is great for telemarketing efforts and can include phone numbers and month/year of birth upon request. Lists can also be double or triple spaced to allow great note-taking room. Lists are normally sorted in zip code order rather than alphabetized by last name but custom sorting should also be available upon request.

## CD-Rom

A CD is a great alternative for customers who want to receive their list digitally but don't have an email address or can't receive larger files via email. CD-ROM's can also be sent in Excel, ASCII or D-Base format.

If you have a product you want to sell to businesses, a business prospecting list can be a great tool for you!

Select by numerous parameters such as employee size, SIC code, years in business and more!

Maximize you direct mail and telemarketing efforts!

Target Your Prime Prospects By:

- Geography (radius, area code, city, county, state, ZIP Code)
- Industry type (SIC Code or Yellow Page Headings)
- Demographics (company size, location type, years in business and more)
- Data on over 14 million U.S. businesses
- THOUSANDS of new businesses added each month

## Accurate and Updated Leads

List should be constantly updated and verified to ensure that your business mailing list always contain the most current, most deliverable addresses and responsive phone numbers available. 100% of your records from the vendor should have been phone verified.

## Specialty List

Sometimes a standard consumer list or business list just won't do. If you have a product that is geared to a specific market, you may need something a little more targeted. Specialty List can help!

## List Types

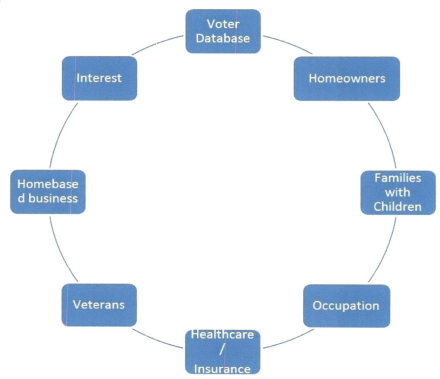

## Voter Database

Over 65 MILLION registered voters available in 20 states by congressional district available to assist you with your next election campaign effort. Within that base, there are approximately 42 million individuals known by their voter party (Republican, Democrat, Independent, and Other/Non-Declared). When used in combination with date of birth and other key lifestyle selects such as "known donor", you have the perfect combination for election and fundraising activities. You can also combine registered voter information with the known homeowner select to target a specific geography that are more likely to turn out at the polls on election day.

## Families with Children

Children influence a large portion of disposable income in a family. Families with young children are perfect prospects for baby items, children's toys, books, clothing, life insurance, magazines, and even college funding. As they get older, parents with pre-teens and teens are more receptive to offers for computers and video games, cell phones, athletic equipment, clothing, and other trendy offers. Families with teens ages 16-18 are prime targets for car insurance, car accessories, electronic equipment, and college offers.

## Homeowners

Owning a home is the American dream. For most families, once the dream comes true, they have to manage ongoing upkeep and improvements to their home. Our Homeowners list is perfect for reaching over 65 million homeowners in need of products and services for their home. They respond to a variety of offers including lawn and garden, pool equipment and chemicals, home furnishings, insurance, electronic equipment, and more. Select by numerous selections such as: home value; mortgage amount; sale date; sale price; home year built; square footage; roof type and more.

## Ethnic/Religion

Different ethnic groups have different interests and lifestyles that warrant culturally targeted offers for travel, foods, telecom products, magazines, newspapers, fundraising, religious offers and more. Ethnic selections also help expand your services to profitable new markets while customizing your message for best response.

## Occupation

An individual's occupation provides insight about interests and activities, disposable income and probable purchase interests. Inferring interests from a job title is a valuable way to target magazine offers, packaged goods, clothing, automobile offers and more. Combining occupation with other demographics provides you with highly targeted segments, and with over 250 occupation indicators, the targeting possibilities are endless.

## Healthcare/Insurance

Whether you sell healthcare services, financial products, insurance or annuities, our database puts you in touch with those most likely to respond to your offer. This database makes it easy to target your most responsive audience whether it is pre-retirees, young families, affluent homeowners, small business owners, or Medicare Supplement prospects. We have the broadest, most accurate coverage of the data elements - such as age, product interest, income, occupation, and home ownership - most critical to your targeting.

## Ailments

Our Ailment database is compiled from consumer-reported health data. This permission-based data was provided directly by mail-responsive consumers via household surveys. Over 82 million consumers can be targeted with this data for more than 100 aches, pains, conditions and treatments. Consumers with ailments are good prospects for products and services that provide them information or relief. They are receptive to appropriately targeted offers that address concerns about their medical needs. Some company and industry restrictions apply.

## Veterans

Connect with America's Veterans who served their country in military service. Displaying their loyalty and patriotism in choosing to serve, most spent time in one of the branches of the American military (Army, Navy, Air Force, Marine Corp, or Coast Guard) during their military service. Many devoted themselves to protecting our freedoms, maintaining peace, providing relief or supporting the U.S. around the globe. Along with the sacrifices of military service come many benefits: training, honor, education, travel, pay and self-discovery, as well as becoming part of a cohesive lifetime community of American servicemen and women. These self-reported households contain current or retired military personnel or indicated an interest in military veterans' affairs. Veterans lists are great prospects for: health and life insurance; donations to vet facilities; donations to injured veterans' associations; investments; employment assistance; travel; and assisted living.

**Interests**

Personal hobbies and interests often drive consumers' discretionary income spending habits. Personal interests often give marketers deeper insight into consumers' spending behavior more than any form of information other than direct consumer feedback. If you need to reach computer users who love motorcycling or fisherman who travel, we have the most comprehensive personal interests' database around. Compiled from the largest collection of detailed surveys and product registration cards available, our database is a premier source of consumer interests and hobbies. With information on how Americans spend their leisure time, you'll target your offers more effectively. Combining these interests can give you an even more finely targeted group of prospects. For example, select people who own pets and are charitable donors to reach consumers who are likely to respond to fundraising requests focused on animal well-being.

**Placing Your Lead Order**

Now that you have taken the time to write a business plan, develop an activity plan and learn about the different type of leads you can use to build your seven-figure business and grow your six-figure income how do you go about creating your lead program?

## Select Lead Type

## Get Counts

## Place Your Order

## Receive Mailed Alerts

## Receive Leads

## Select Lead Types

**Medicare (Supplement, Advantage)**

We don't have to tell you about the number of people turning 65 between now and 2030, but it's a lot.

Turning 65 leads are a must.

Solid response rates with interested parties equate to a repeatable and profitable market solution. Set up an order cycle every month or build a quarterly plan to ensure that you continue to receive a steady flow of boomers aging into Medicare.

Over 65 Medicare Supplement leads cannot be overlooked. There are so many Americans paying more than they need to. They understand the process. They are NOT bombarded with mail. If you sell one of the top two lowest carriers in your market, this is a remarkable marketing tool.

Dual Eligible mailings are generally top performers. Response rates average 4.5%. These people want and need help. You're just the person they are looking for.

Regardless if you are new to Medicare Supplement or are a seasoned veteran, direct mail leads work. They are 100% Exclusive and ideal for both field and remote agents.

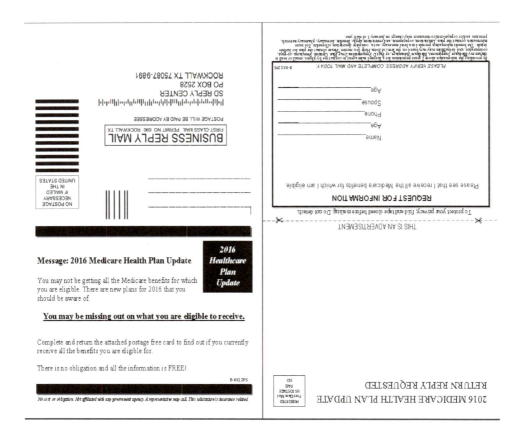

## Final Expense

Final expense direct mail lead programs are ideal for reaching prospects interested in plans that cover their burial expenses so they avoid leaving their loved ones with a financial burden and stress. Typical response rates on the most popular final expense leads are around 1.5%-2% average nationally! Many agents report converting as much as 33% of final expense leads. These consumers are concerned about this issue and need agents to guide them through the process.

Order leads that are not preprinted so you can easily customize the wording to meet your own needs.

The lists need to be updated monthly and verified through multiple sources to ensure the highest quality and deliverability. Households mailed are not re-mailed for 90 days regardless of the mail piece used.

We recommend ages 50-75, estimated household income under $50,000 and excluding PO Boxes when targeting your final expense direct mail lead campaign but you can choose any demographics that you prefer.

Consider ordering leads that are EXCLUSIVELY yours. You may want leads that are resold that are received back from mailings you pay for.

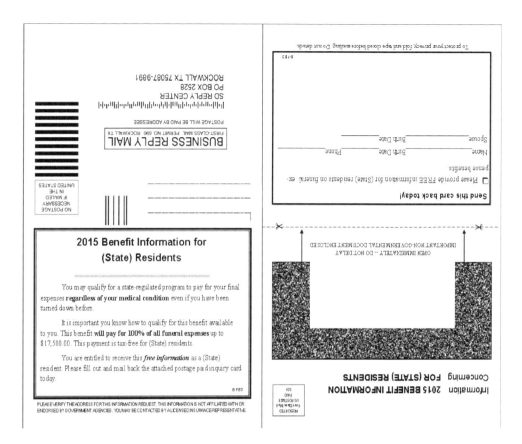

## Long-Term Care Insurance

Use vendors that have a number of Long-Term Care lead samples available that average between .5% and 1.5%. Use mailers that are NOT preprinted so you can easily customize the text on our mailers to fit your needs.

TargetLeads® are also the ONLY direct mail lead vendor contracted with the state of California and the state of Louisiana.

## Annuity

Use annuity leads to target baby boomers and seniors. Annuity mailers without a gift offer typically have a response rate of about .2% to .5%. We have combination leads that offer a check box for annuity information that usually generate 1.5% to 3%. Our recommended selections are ages 55-75 with an annual household income of $75K plus.

## Combination

One of the most effective ways to market multiple products is a combination lead mailer. If you sell Medicare Supplements, Long-Term Care, Final Expense and even Annuities... a combination lead may be just right for you! Average response rates on combination leads range from 1.5% to over 4% depending on the state mailed.

Combination leads can be customized to include other products that you offer. Ancillary products that have added "areas of interest" check boxes for products such as Dental, Vision, Prescription Discounts, Home Health Care, Cancer Insurance, Accidental Death, Critical Illness and more.

**Custom**

Whether you are wanting to mail a four-color jumbo postcard, a personalized letter with reply piece in an envelope, or a color trifold mailer, use a vendor that can do it all for you.

Get a quote on a custom mailing, including details such as: preferred paper type, do you want it to mail 1st class or bulk, does it self-mail or need an outgoing envelope, etc.

Using a One Stop Shop vendor means you could also get other printed items such as business cards, magnets, door hangers, flyers, brochures, letterhead and more!

## Get Counts

Select your cities/zips, counties or SCF's. Choose names demographically by age, income, dwelling type, gender, marital status, ethnicity, homeowners, etc. use vendors that offer the ability to Run Your Counts Online.

## Place Your Order

With most vendors, you can call in your order, fax it, email it or even use our online order form - whichever is most convenient for you. Payment is required up front and most vendors accept check, money order or credit card (accepted is AMEX, MC, Visa, and Discover).

## Receive Mailed Alerts

Utilize a vendor who will, after you place your order, provide an email alert when your order has been mailed. Lead orders are usually mailed within three to five business days. Responses normally start coming in within 1 ½ to 2 weeks from mail date.

## Receive Leads

TargetLeads are uploaded daily AT NO ADDITIONAL CHARGE for you to login, view and print (or save to your computer) or into TL LeadManager® for contact management. Leads can also be mailed once a week (usually on Tuesdays) with special shipping available upon request.

**Every Door Direct Mail Lead**

Attract all the clients your business can handle with Every Door Direct Mail.

• Build more traffic by finding new customers.
• No mailing list required.
• Oversized mailers grab attention.
• Mail as few as 200 or up to 5,000 per day.
• Target address at carrier route level for better responses.
• We prepare all postal paperwork, sort, mail and deliver to USPS.
• We can help you increase your revenue.
• Ask about all of your options and opportunities!

You can reach **EVERY** home - **EVERY** address - **EVERY** time!

# CHAPTER 3 -- CONTACT MANAGEMENT SYSTEM

TL LeadManager® is a lead management system designed exclusively for Life and Health Insurance Agents.

This prospecting database housed in your own contact management system, TL LeadManager® which contains vital information about prospects that have been contacted through your lead orders.

By returning leads after you have worked them, and including important information, you help develop and improve your prospecting database.

One crucial piece of information you can provide is the prospect's current insurance provider. With this information, you can build a list of prospects for any specific competitor.

These Database Leads can be accessed by you whenever a competing company experiences a large rate increase, stops offering a product in your area, or makes some other change that encourages their prospects to consider other insurance options.

Managing your Medicare Supplement, Long Term Care, Final Expense and Annuity leads has never been easier. If you don't have or don't love your current lead/contact management system, you need to check out TL LeadManager®!

This feature rich, easy to use contact management system, CRM, is designed to minimize the time you spend working leads and maximize your selling time.

Reduce your paperwork, be more organized than ever before and start selling more policies. Used in conjunction with TargetLeads® they can make your direct mail marketing efforts as seamless as possible.

Whether using Turning 65 lists for Medicare Supplement or any other kind of insurance leads, TLLM will allow you to manage, follow-up and run reports on all of your campaigns.

Managing ROI is always tricky to compute. You have to be diligent on inputting your sales and non-sales. TL LeadManager® is designed so that these important portions of your reporting are inherent into how the system works. Managing your follow-up and ROI has never been easier.

Whether you are focused on Medicare supplement leads, final expense leads, long-term care leads, annuity leads or turning 65 lists, TargetLeads' TL LeadManager® is built to save you time and make you money.

TL LeadManager® software will help you work smarter and more efficiently. In today's marketplace that is essential to survival.

## Complete Lead Intelligence at Your Fingertips

TL LeadManager® is about knowing who, what, when and where. With TLLM you can view all customer transactions, respond confidently to customer calls or emails, capture important information about customer interactions and manage your tasks and follow-up activities. In addition, all direct mail lead responses from TargetLeads® include the scanned image of the returned card and is data entered for you to view immediately.

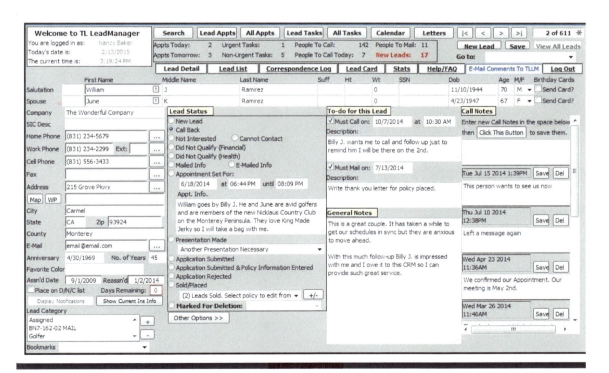

## Organize and Track Prospects and Clients

With countless ways for you to access lead information and tools for you to disposition, track and follow-up available for you to use in managing your business, no opportunities are lost. With a few clicks you can view who needs your attention each day, your last conversation and the disposition of each and every prospect and client.

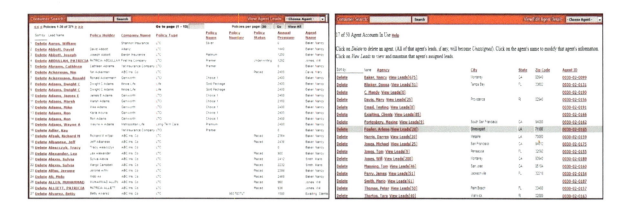

## Custom Cards to Stay in Front of Your Clients

Integrated seamlessly into TL LeadManager® is the ability to send high quality customized cards to your prospects and clients. Send a "Thank You!" card for setting an appointment, new policy or a referral. Approximately 40% of all insurance is sold around birthdays – send your prospects and clients a birthday card and get their business.

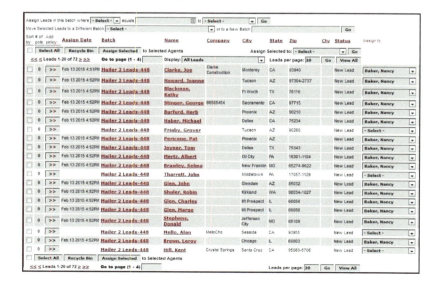

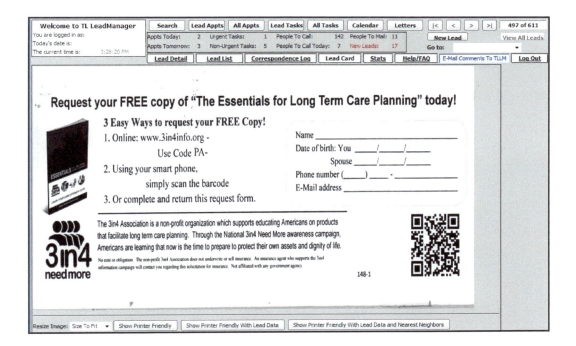

## Features Galore

TL LeadManager® is full of features to help you sell more policies while spending less time working your leads. Driving directions, commission tracking, letter writing and single click sales reporting are only just a few of the features available. Maximize your marketing dollars by utilizing everything TLLM has to offer.

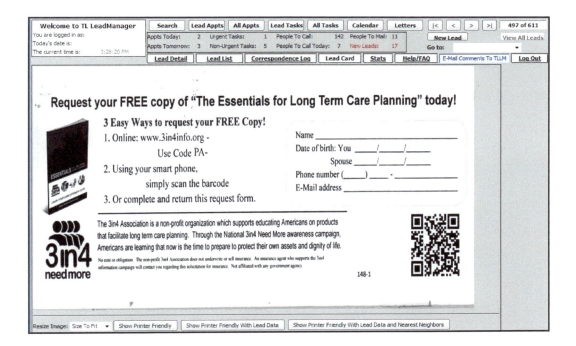

## Custom Cards

Sending customized "Thank You and Birthday Cards is integrated into TL LeadManager® making it quick and easy to stay in front of your prospects and clients. Maximize your marketing dollars by utilizing everything TLLM has to offer.

# CHAPTER 4 - PHONE TIPS AND SCRIPTS

| | |
|---|---|
| **Basic Phone Approach Tips** | Let's review some basic telephone tips:<br><br>Be prepared—there's no substitute for this step<br><br>Be brief—remember, most Americans are "time poor"<br><br>Be enthusiastic—it is contagious<br><br>Be urgent—you want the message to be perceived as important<br><br>Talk a little faster than normal<br><br>Talk a little louder than normal<br><br>Talk a little clearer than normal<br><br>When you make your phone calls:<br><br>Have a calendar<br><br>Have a map<br><br>Have your phone script<br><br>Have your rebuttals prepared<br><br>Call for a set period of time<br><br>Set a call goal<br><br>Don't quit until you reach your goal |
| **Tips** | Don't accept interruptions. You are running a business and everyone around you will only respect your business when you demonstrate respect for your business.<br><br>Remember the goal is to sell the appointment, not a product.<br><br>Don't answer product/price questions; sell the appointment.<br><br>The most successful prospectors keep their approach simple and to the point, allowing the prospect's only objection to be in meeting them personally. It's difficult for anyone to reject another person! |

| | |
|---|---|
| **Preparing to use Phone Scripts** | Your sales methodology, like the phone script for setting appointments, should use a series of questions to gain commitment and ensure understanding. There are some proven techniques for setting appointments that reinforce this.<br><br>Here are the Five Rules for Setting Appointments from Earl Nightingale:<br><br>1. Always use "please" and "thank you"<br>2. Use the customer's name five times in the conversation<br>3. Identify yourself and your company<br>4. State your purpose for the call<br>5. Close with a question<br><br>Let's review how these are used for setting appointments.<br><br>Now you'll get to put the Five Rules into action by creating your own script. Once you write your script, practice it by presenting it to your team or manager through role-play. |
| **Using Your Phone Script** | Learning effective phone skills takes practice, so to help you get started; here is a Phone Script job aid. |
| **Calling off a Survey Card** | Good morning/afternoon, Mr./Mrs._____. This is _____ with [company name]. I was in last week doing a survey and you said you were interested in saving money on [product/service/plan]. (DON'T PAUSE!!)<br><br>To see if you qualify, I will have to ask you a couple of questions and then set a time to meet. (ASK QUALIFYING QUESTIONS)<br><br>I have a time open at _____ or _____. Which is best for you?<br><br>Alright, we will be meeting on (Date) at (Time) at (location). My name is _____. That's (give spelling). Would you write that down on your calendar? Oh, by the way, have your [contract, invoices, or bills] with you for the appointment. Have a nice day! |
| **Calling off a Referral** | I'm _____ with [company name]. I met with (client's name) last week and was able to save him some money on his [product/service/plan]. He mentioned you might be interested in saving money too. (DON'T PAUSE!!)<br><br>To see if you qualify, I'll have to ask you a couple of questions and then set a time to meet. (ASK QUALIFYING QUESTIONS)<br><br>I have a time open at _____ or _____. Which is best for you?<br><br>Alright, we will be meeting on (Date) at (Time) at (location). My name is _____. That's (give spelling). Would you write that down on your calendar? Oh, by the way, have your [contract/agreement/invoice] with you for the appointment. Have a nice day! |
| **Using Take Ones to Set** | Another tool from the Wheel of Fortune approach to prospecting is the use of Take One flyers. These scripting techniques let you maximize your prospecting potential when you introduce yourself and ask to leave Take |

| | |
|---|---|
| *Appointments* | One flyers at a business.<br><br>Remember, your approach is to ask a series of questions to get results. The script will guide you into asking questions to successfully place and get leads from a Take One. |
| *Take One Presentation Script* | Ask: "Can I leave this here?" as you bring in the Take One boxes.<br><br>Response to Business Owner:<br>"You must be the owner." When the owner asks, "What is it?" begin the script:<br><br>"This is a new kind of [product/service/plan]. A lot of people have [describe product/service/replacing/offering] and you have pretty [describe problem/cost/lack of service of competitor product/service/plan].<br><br>"This is a [state three benefits of your product/service/plan for the business owner's customers].<br><br>"Let me ask you—Do you have the old kind or the new kind of [product/service/plan]?<br><br>"Well let me ask you—if we could get you qualified [of course you have to qualify to get this kind product/service/plan] if we could get you qualified with [describe benefit of product/service] you'd be interested in looking at this for you and your [business/team/family], wouldn't you?"<br><br>"Can I leave this here?"<br><br>(Leave Take One box). |
| *Survey Scripting* | Like using Take Ones, surveying is another way for that important face-to face sales approach. Take time finding an area with many potential small business prospects to ask questions. |

| | |
|---|---|
| **Survey Script** | "I'm doing a survey of small business owners. Do you mind if I ask you a few questions?"<br><br>Are you either self-employed or the owner? _____<br><br>How many years have you been in business? _____<br><br>Do you have any employees? If yes, how many? _____<br><br>Do you belong to any associations that offer savings and benefits to your business? If Yes, which associations? _____<br><br>Who covers your [your product/service]? _____<br><br>Would you like to receive information on our [your product/service] for small businesses, which features [state three benefits of your product/service] and offers substantial cost savings?<br>_____<br><br>If "yes," you're done!<br><br>If "no," ask:<br><br>What would cause you to consider changing your present plan?<br><br>  Better price stability? _____<br><br>  More benefits for the same cost? _____<br><br>  Same benefits for less _____<br><br>  Better financial protection? _____<br><br>  Company strength and customer service? _____<br><br>If "Better Price Stability and Financial Protection?" or "More benefits for the same cost" were available to you…would you be willing to visit with a local representative at some point in the future?<br>_____<br><br>Name of Business: _____<br>Name of Owner: _____<br>Street: _____<br>City: _____ State:_____ Zip:_____<br>Phone #: _____ Best time to call:_____<br>Name of Representative: _____ |

| | |
|---|---|
| **Using Business Cards** | This is another technique for approaching small business owners. Like the other scripting techniques, you're constantly asking questions to gather information and gain interest by the prospect. |
| **Business Card Approach** | "Hi, how are you today?  My name is_____ and I am looking for the owner of the business?<br><br>"Thank you.<br><br>"Look, I'm with a local [your business or service company] and I have some clients I was visiting in this area so I thought I'd stop by, introduce myself, and exchange business cards with you.  Would that be all right?  Great.  By the way, when is usually a good time to reach you—morning or evening?<br><br>Early in the week or later in the week?<br><br>Thanks.<br>(On the way out of the business, ask)<br><br>"You do have [your product/service], don't you?  Would you say you're paying more than you wanted or more than you expected for that?"<br><br>"I'll give you a call and set up a time when we could take a minute or two and see if we share a common philosophy concerning [your product/service]. |
| **Two Approaches for Setting Appointments** | There are two approaches for setting the appointment:<br>Direct Approach<br>Phone Approach<br>The only purpose of each approach is to set the appointment with the suspect.  No one to talk to equals no chance to make money.  You transform suspects into prospects through qualification.  The most valuable asset you have is a prospect.  Each prospect you help buy must be replaced.<br><br>The Direct approach is easier for some because they feel the rejection rate is lower than the Phone approach.  As you learn and practice the techniques, determine which approach is best for you. |
| **Version 1: Lead Card in Hand** | "Good morning/afternoon, Mr./Mrs._____.  My name is _____. I'm here in response to your request for more information on [state product/service] offered through [your company name]. (DON'T PAUSE!!!)<br><br>"To see if you qualify, I'll have to ask you a couple of questions, and then set a time to meet. (ASK QUALIFYING QUESTIONS)<br><br>"I have time open at _____ or _____.  Which is best for you?<br><br>"All right, we will be meeting on _____ at _____, your home |

| | |
|---|---|
| | address. My name is _____, that's _____ (give spelling). Would you write that down on your calendar? Please have your [contract, invoice, billings] with you for our appointment?<br><br>"By the way, Mr./Mrs._____, who owns the business next door?<br><br>"Thank you; have a nice day." |
| **Version 2: Lead Card in Hand** | "Hello, may I speak with (Customer's Full Name) please?<br><br>"(Customer's Full Name)? Thank you! (Customer's First Name), my name is (your name) and I'm with [your company name]. Recently, you requested information on our affordable [your product/service] and (Customer's First Name) the reason I stopped by is just to let you know I'm going to be in the area this week and I can see you at (Day) at (Time). Will you be in then?<br><br>"(If No) When will you be in?<br><br>"Great! Before I take off, let me ask you a few quick questions. (ASK QUALIFYING QUESTIONS)<br><br>"Thank you, (Customer's First Name). I'll see you on (Date) at (Time)." |

**Direct Mail Response Card**

"Hello, my name is [state your name]."

"I've recently been assigned the [mention city, county or market] area by [company/your name here]."

"I'm calling in response to your recent request concerning [your product/service]."

"I have here that your full name is [state prospects name] and that your correct address is [state address here]. Is that correct?"

**Small Business List**

"Hello, my name is [state your name]."

"I've recently been transferred by my company, [your company name here], to the [mention city, county or market] area."

"I'm calling to introduce myself and to offer you a FREE, no-obligation [review/evaluation/estimate] on your [your product/service]."

"Who do you currently have [your product/service] with?"

"Hello, my name is [state your name] with [your company name here]."

"We've recently introduced the [your product/service here] to the [mention city, county or market] market."

"These [your product/service/plans] allow for not only [your product/service primary feature], but also are designed with [your product/service/plan primary benefit] to those who qualify."

"Are you at all familiar with the [your exclusive product/service/plan]?"

**New Business Leads**

"Hello, my name is [state name]."

"I noticed that you have recently opened a new company in the [state industry] business."

"How does it feel to be a new business owner [state prospects name]?"

"Well, [state prospects name], I'm with [your company name here] and I specialize in the self-employed market."

"Are you currently [your product/service/plan] or do you still have [product/service/plan]?"

### SO, YOU'VE GOT THE APPOINTMENT

Once you have set the appointment,

YOU SHOULD:

    a.   Anticipate the close

    a.   Prepare yourself for the close

    a.   <u>Prepare your prospect for the close</u>

**Sample One**

"Now, [state prospects name] nobody likes surprises.

So, before I see you on [state appointment date] I'll need you to do the following.

If I'm able to [design a product/service/plan] that meets the needs of yourself and you're [company/team/family]…TO GET YOUR PLAN STARTED …

I'll need [billings/invoices/maintenance records/decision makers], and a listing [current supplier/server company/products in use].

I'll go over the [use/history/projections/needs] required to come up with a pretty accurate price for you but I'll need the authorization from all [stakeholders/owners/decision makers] for [their company name here] to verify the right solution is being provided.

We will then simply [whatever your contract/payment process is] and I'll submit the answers to the [fact finder/survey form/meeting requirements] to our [your accounting/approval/boss] for their review."

"Understand that you have **NO MONEY** at risk.

If for some reason you were not to [approved/qualify] for the [your product/service], the company will refund your money…

You did say your company is looking to grow in the near future, didn't you…
Now, let me again confirm the time of the appointment as [state date and time of the appointment] at your [state home or business] located at [repeat address]."

Is that correct?  Good I look forward to seeing you then."

**Sample Two**

"Now, [state prospect's name], it sounds like we are the perfect fit.

I can tell that you are serious about getting this handled**, IS THAT CORRECT?** …

 It also sounds like you are a very busy man/woman, **SO AM** I.

However, due to the **QUALITY** of our [products/service/plans] and my ability to design a specific [product/service/plan] to meet your needs, I'm 99% sure that we will be able to determine if you [qualify/fit/need] to [apply/upgrade/extend] on [state appointment date] when we meet.

Does that sound **GOOD** to you? …

Once we have decided on the [product/service/plan] that best meets your needs, we will then complete the [contract/application/agreement] and send it to our [manager/accounting/company] with a check for the first month's [service/payment] for their review.

I will need [authorization/schedule/meeting] for all [users/departments/employees] to be [using/servicing/covered] to review and answer their questions.

I look forward to meeting you on [state appointment date] at [state appointment time].

I'm sure you will be relieved to have this handled and out of the way."

# REFERRAL MARKETING

Obtaining a referral or introduction from someone you know to someone you don't know is your best source for getting solid leads. When you are successful in obtaining referrals, or getting an introduction you not only strengthen the current relationship, but also get leads for starting new relationships.

## Advantages of referrals

a. Referral prospecting is the most efficient, therefore least frustrating of all methods.
b. It is a closing activity and needs a practiced, rehearsed track for efficiency
c. You spend more time selling than prospecting

## Timing is Important

Asking for referrals at the correct psychological moment when the client is most enthusiastic about what you've done for him will increase the referrals you get.

Get referrals at the time you have the greatest influence over your prospect

- After the contract/application/order has been signed

- At the time of product/service delivery/installation/implementation

- At a service call

## *Ask for names not leads.*

Develop future contacts by asking them to think of people they know who belong to organizations, such as:

- Kiwanis

- Rotary

- Neighborhood councils

- Church affiliations

- School systems

- Immediate or extended family

Think back before you were in the insurance or financial service business, when you were in another profession.

How many people came to you and ask "Hey John, who do you know I can buy [product name here, life, health, annuity, etc.]?"

My guess is most of you will answer "no-one", yet we are trained in this business to ask a question, specifically designed to illicit a response of "I don't know anyone."

Agent: "John my business is built on referrals so who do you know what I can help or save money with their [product name here, life insurance, health insurance, annuity, etc.}?"

Client: "I don't know anyone." Or "I can't think of anyone but I'll let you know."

Isn't that the most common answer you get, and this is the biggest reason agents more often than not don't get referrals.

However, when you ask for an introduction, rather than ask "who" questions you often will get a name. Or when you attach a behavior to a request you get a name, let's look at how this could work.

### *Key Phrase for* the Referral
"[client's name] you mentioned that your son lives in the area and in fact runs his own auto repair shop in town.

If he walked in here right now would you introduce me?

Would you feel comfortable telling him you feel like I did a good job for you today?

Is there any reason I could not tell him that?

Great, what is his phone number?"

Additional referrals may come in the form of answers to the following behavior questions.

- *Who do you know who has just…?*
    - Moved here from out of town?
    - Bought a new home?
    - Started a new job?
    - Established his or her business?
    - Married or become engaged?
    - Had a new baby?
    - Started a youngster in school?
    - Achieved retirement age?
    - Gone on an association committee?

## Getting Referral reminders:

- Get names first - don't interrupt.

- If a person does not buy - you get paid in two ways, a sale or a referral - ask for a referral

- Make asking for a referral a habit

### Suggested Phrase when approaching a Referral:

"Mr./Mrs. (Referral), I have no way of knowing if I can be of benefit to you, but (Prospect) feels I was able to provide help to him.

I would like to get together with you and show you what I would do similar to what I have done for [client's name]."

## Referral Reminders:

1. *Give feedback to the referrer. People want to know what happened.*

2. *Let your referrer know in advance that obtaining referrals is part of how you get paid.*

3. *Never throw away a referral. The timing may be off and he/she may be in the market at some future date.*

4. *Research shows that the more you call a given list of prospects, the better your results become.*

And remember when you **attach a behavior** to a request you usually **get a name**!

## Survey Script

"I am surveying small business owners in the area about the rising cost and declining benefits of [your product/service] locally. May I ask you a few questions? It will only take 60 seconds. If you purchased your current [product/service] in order to [feature/benefit] against the risk of [feature/benefit loss], <u>YOU MAY STILL BE AT RISK</u>

1. Are you either self – employed or the owner?

2. How many years have you been in business?

3. Do you have any employees? If yes, how many?

4. Do you belong to any associations that offer savings and benefits to your business? If yes, which associations?

5. Who covers your [product/service]?

6. Would you like to receive information on our [your product/service/plan] for small businesses, which features one year [price/cost/rate] guarantee and may offer substantial cost savings? If "yes" YOU'RE DONE! If "NO" go to #7

7. What would cause you to consider changing your present [product/service]?
    a. Better [price/cost/rate] stability?
    b. More benefits for the same cost?
    c. Same benefits for less cost?
    d. Better financial protection?
    e. Company strength/company service?

8. If "Better [price/cost/rate] stability and financial protection" or "More benefits for the same cost" were available to you … would you be willing to visit with a local representative at some point in the future?

Name of Business: _____

Name of Owner: _____

Address: _____ City: _____ State: _____ Zip: _____

Best time to call: _____

Name of sales person: _____

## BUSINESS CARD APPROACH

"Hi [prospect's name].

How are you today?

My name is [your name here] and I'm with [your company].

Has anyone from our office been in to see you yet?

Very quickly, let me tell you why I stopped by. [your company name] offers free quotes on [product/service/plan]; we have the [your product/service/plan] plans. Do you feel you are paying too much for medical coverage?"

"What company is your current [product/service] with?

Your monthly [cost/payment/price] how much?

We may be able to help! (Be emphatic)"

"Mr./Mrs. [prospect's name], I can't talk to you right now, but I'll get back to you as soon as I can. Do you have a business card?"

**OR**

"I'm [your name here] with [your company name]. I've been talking to other small business owners like you. Are you currently covered by a [product/service] program?"

(If Yes) – "Then are you interested in saving money on your [product/service/plan]?"

(If No) – "I can't stay now, but I'll be back with you in a few days. Do you have a business card?"

(If No) – "Is there any particular reason you haven't looked at a program thus far?" or "Would you be interested in investing 15 minutes to allow me to show you a plan that may be more affordable?"

(If Yes) – "I can't stay now, but I'll be back with you in a few days. Do you have a business card?" *On your way out, ask:* By the way, when is the best time to call you? Are you in on Mondays? Great! I'll call you Monday at ---: ----"

**OR**

"Hi, how are you today?

My name is [your name here] and I am looking for the owner of the business.
Thank you."

**Alternative Business Card Approach**

"Look, I'm with [your company name here] and I have some clients I was visiting in this area so I thought I'd stop by, introduce myself and exchange business cards with you.

Would that be all right?

Great!

By the way, when is a usually god time to reach you?

I'll give you a call and set up a time where we could take a minute or two and see if we share a common philosophy concerning [product/service/plan].

Fair enough?"

**SETTING THE APPOINTMENT**

There are two approaches for setting the appointments:
- Direct Approach
- Phone Approach

The only purpose of each approach is to set the appointment with the prospect.

No one to talk to equals any chance to sell.

You transform prospects into clients through qualification.
The most valuable asset you have is a prospect.

Each prospect you sell must be replaced!

The Direct approach is easier because the rejection rate can be lower than the phone approach.

It is easier for a prospect to say he's too busy, not interested or to simply hang up when using the phone than when you're standing in front of them.

## DIRECT APPROACH SCRIPTS

### Script 1: Lead Card in Hand

"Good morning/afternoon, Mr./Mrs. [prospect name].

My name is [your name here].

I'm here in response to your request for more information about either increasing your current [product/service/plan] benefits or lowering your cost. (Don't Pause)

To see if you/ what you would qualify for, I'll have to ask you a couple of questions and then set a time to meet."

(Ask qualifying questions)

"I have time open on [name a day of the week] at [state a time]. Which is best for you?

All right, we will be meeting on..."
(repeat the appointment date agreed to), at [confirm the prospect's address].

"My name is [your name], that's [give spelling].

Would you write that down on your calendar?

Please have your [contract/agreement/policy] with you for our appointment.

By the way, Mr./Mrs. [prospect's name here], who owns the business next door?"

### Script 2: Lead Card in Hand

"Hello, may I speak with [state prospect's name] please?

[state prospects name].

Thank you!

[state prospect's name], my name is [your name] and I'm with [your company name here].

Recently you requested information on our [product/service] and [state prospects name], the reason I'm stopping by is just to let you know I'm going to be in the area this week and I can see you [state a day and time]. Will you be in then?"

(If No) – "When will you be in?"

"Great!

Before I take off, let me ask you a few quick questions."
(ask the basic qualifying questions)

"Thank you, [state prospects name].

I'll see you on [state agreed appointment date and time]"

## PHONE APPROACH SCRIPT

**APPROACH**: *The act of contacting a prospect either in person or by phone and requesting a meeting. The use of a carefully crafted script comprised of a few well-chosen words has proven to be the most effective method of making appointments.*

*The objective of the approach is to secure an appointment with the prospect. This should be your only focus during the phone approach step. Attempting to sell a product or service during the approach will hurt your chances for success.*

*A key point to keep in mind is that any time you mention a product, a service or a price during your approach; you are giving your prospect something to object to!*

*The most successful prospectors keep their approach simple and to the point, allowing the prospect's only objection to be in meeting them personally. It's difficult for anyone to reject another person!*

*Here are a few sample telephone approaches:*

"Hello, may I speak with [prospect's name] please?

[Prospects name]?

Thank You.

[Prospects name], my name is [your name] and I'm with [your company name here].

Recently, [prospect's name], you requested information on our [your product/service/plan] and the reason I'm calling is just to let you know I'm going to be in your area this week and [prospect's name] I have time to bring this by [state day and time].

 Will you be in?"

If "NO" ... Ask, "When will you be in?"

*After appointment is set, confirm the address and zip code get directions and ask the following qualifying questions: (Seal the Appointment)*

"Great!

Before I hang up I need to ask you a few quick questions,"

- You have [product/service/plan] now, don't you? If "NO", ask "Why?"
- Who is that with?
- How much are you paying for that [product/service]?
- Is the [feature/benefit] for you and your family or for your whole business?
- Will you be [covering/servicing] any [subsidiary's/employees/children]?
- Do either of you use [knock out questions]?
- Are there any [knock out conditions/situations]?
- Is anyone currently [looking/getting bids/pricing]?
- Your [decision maker/other decision makers] will be there when I come by, won't he/she?

"Thank you [prospect's name]. I'll see you on [agreed appointment day and time]"

## CALLING OFF SURVEY CARD

"Good morning/afternoon, Mr./Mrs. [prospect name].

This is [your name] with [your company name here].

I was in last week doing a survey and you said you were interested in saving money on your [product/service/plan]." (Don't pause)

"To see if you qualify, I will have to ask you a couple of questions.

I have a time open [state a day and time] or [state a day and time].

Which is best for you?

Alright, we will be meeting on [state agreed appointment date/time] at [repeat location].

My name is [your name].

That's [give spelling]. Would you write that down on your calendar?

Oh, by the way, have your [contract/agreement/policy] with you for the appointment please.

Have a nice day."

## CALLING OFF A REFERRAL

"I'm [your name] with [your company name here].

I met with [referrers name] last week and was able to save him/her some money on his/her [product/service/plan].

He/she mentioned you might be interested in saving money too. (DON'T PAUSE)

I have a time open at [state a day and time] or [state a day and time].

Which is best for you?

Alright, we will be meeting on [state agreed appointment day and time] at [repeat location].

My name is [your name].

That's [spell your name].

Would you write that down on your calendar?

Oh, by the way, have your [contract/agreement/policy] with you for the appointment please.

Have a nice day."

## Medicare Supplement Phone Script

Opening: "Good morning, is this Mr./Ms. [----------------]?

Mr./Ms. [---------------], this is [salesperson's name] with [agency name].

I am calling you about your Medicare supplement.

I am assuming that you already have a Medicare supplement. Is that correct?"

1. "The purpose of my call is to make sure that you are not paying too much for your supplemental insurance. Do you have a moment to talk?"

   **Or**

   "The purpose of my call is to make sure that you are not paying more than $------- for your supplemental insurance. Do you have a moment to talk?"

2. "Are you currently paying for your own insurance or do you have this as a retirement benefit from your former employer?"

3. "It doesn't hurt to review from time to time the premium that you are paying".

   **Or**

   "I want to give you something to compare your premium with."

4. If you don't mind telling me your age, I can give you an accurate premium comparison. Or "If you don't mind confirming your age (birthday), I can give you more specific information."

5. Are you paying too much for your Medicare coverage?

6. "Do you want the same coverage for a lower premium?  Medicare Supplements are regulated so the benefits from each plan are the same.  You have identical benefits no matter how much you pay for it.  You <u>can</u> pay more, but you don't <u>get</u> more – you get the <u>same thing</u>."

   **Or**

   "It is important to have a Medicare supplement policy, but it is equally important not to pay more than you have to for the same coverage.  Medicare Supplements are regulated so the benefits from each plan are the same.  You have identical benefits no matter how much you pay for it.  You can <u>pay</u> more, but you don't <u>get</u> more – you get the <u>same thing</u>."

7. (after giving them the comparison) "Hopefully that is lower, and if it is, I would like to meet with you and give you complete information on our products.

   Would (Monday or Tuesday) be better for you?"


**Close and stay closed.**

**Senior Product Telephone Script**

**Opening A:** "Hello, Mr./Ms. [--------------], this is [--------------] with [agency name]. I am calling to offer you a free comparison on Medicare supplement insurance. You can use the comparison information to compare with what you currently have, to see if you might be able to save some money on your insurance premium cost. There is absolutely no obligation to the offer. Is this a convenient time?"
(*If response is yes, go to B. If response is No, go to C.*)

**Opening A1**: "Hello, Mr./Ms. [--------------], this is [--------------] with [agency name]. The purpose of my call today is to offer you information about our Long-Term Care insurance coverage. We have plans with benefits that allow you to stay in your own home & receive care. There is absolutely no obligation to the offer. Is this a convenient time?"
(*If response is yes, go to B1. If response is No, go to C.*)

**Opening A2**: "Hello, Mr./Ms. [--------------], this is[ --------------] with [agency name]. The purpose of my call today is to offer you information about our Final Expense Life insurance. Have you made arrangements for final expenses? We have a very competitive plan. I can have one of our local representatives provide you with a comparison. There is absolutely no obligation to the offer. Is this a convenient time?"
(*If response is yes, go to B2. If response is No, go to C.*)

**B.** "I just need to verify your address and date of birth. Mr./Ms. [--------------], I am showing your address as [---------------]. Is that correct? And your date of birth is? Do you currently have a Medicare supplement policy?"
(*If response is yes, go to D. If on an HMO plan, go to J or K. If response is No, go to E.*)

**B1**. "I just need to verify your address and date of birth. Mr./Ms. [--------------], I am showing your address as [--------------]. Is that correct? And your date of birth is?"
(*If response is Yes, interested in receiving information, go to Close 1. If response is No, already have a plan, go to L. If response is No, not interested, go to K.*)

**B2**: "I just need to verify your address and date of birth. Mr./Ms. [--------------], I am showing your address as [--------------]. Is that correct? And your date of birth is?
(*If response is Yes, interested in receiving information, go to Close 1. If response is No, already have a plan, go to L. If response is No, not interested, go to J.*)

**C.** "Would tomorrow or [--------------] be more convenient?" (Note day and time.)
"Great, I'll call back then." *(Go to Close 3.)*

**D.** "Do you pay the premium"? *(If response is Yes, go to F. If response is No, on an employer-paid plan, go to J or I. If response is No, on an HMO plan, go to J or K. If response is No, on Medicaid program, go to Close 4.)*

**E.** "When do you plan on enrolling in Medicare?" *(If response is less than 6 months, go to G. If response is more than 6 months, set as a future contact and go to Close 3.)*

**F.** "What company is your current coverage with?" *(Record response)* "What do you like most about your current coverage? What do you dislike about your current coverage? Which plan do you currently have?" *(Go to H.)*

**G.** "Now is the ideal time to consider Medicare supplement insurance. Let me have one of our local representatives provide you with a comparison?"
*(If response is <u>yes</u>, go to Close 1. If response is <u>No</u>, go to Close 2.)*

**H.** "Why don't I have one of our local representatives give you a comparison?"
*(If response is <u>yes</u>, go to Close 1. If response is <u>No</u>, go to Close 2.)*

**I.** "That's great. We are finding that most employer plans do not include coverage for nursing home stays. We have plans with benefits that allow you to stay in your own home and receive care. I can have one of our local representatives provide you with a comparison for this type of coverage." *(If response is <u>yes</u>, go to Close 1. If response is <u>No</u>, go to Close 2.)*

**J.** "We find that people who are at or near retirement age are concerned about the high cost of nursing home stays. We have plans with benefits that allow you to stay in your own home and receive care. I can have one of our local representatives provide you with a comparison for this type of coverage." *(If response is <u>Yes</u>, go to Close 1. If response is <u>No</u>, go to Close 2.)*

**K.** "Have you made plans for final expenses? We have a very competitive Final Expense Life insurance plan. I can have one of our local representatives provide you with a comparison." *(If response is <u>Yes</u>, go to Close 1. If response is <u>No</u>, go to Close 2.)*

**L.** "You know, it never hurts to compare. We may be able to save you some money on your premium cost, so why don't I have one of our local representatives contact you with a (comparison) or (information)?" *(If response is <u>Yes</u>, go to Close 1. If response is <u>No</u>, go to Close 2.)*

**M.** "If we could save you money on your premium costs, would you be interested?" *(If response is <u>Yes</u>, go to Close 1. If response is <u>No</u>, go to Close 2.)*

**Close 1.** "Okay, one of our local representatives will contact you within the next seven to 10 days with your (comparison) or (information). Thank you for your time today. Good-bye."

**Close 2.** "Mr./Mrs.[--------------], Thank you for your time today. Good-bye".

**Close 3.** "Okay, great. We will call you back on [--------------]. Mr./Mrs. [--------------], Thank you for your time today. Good-bye."

**Close 4.** "I am sorry, but we are not able to help you at this time. Mr./Mrs. --------------, Thank you for your time today. Good-bye."

*Face to Face*
*Contact Means*
*Greater Sales*

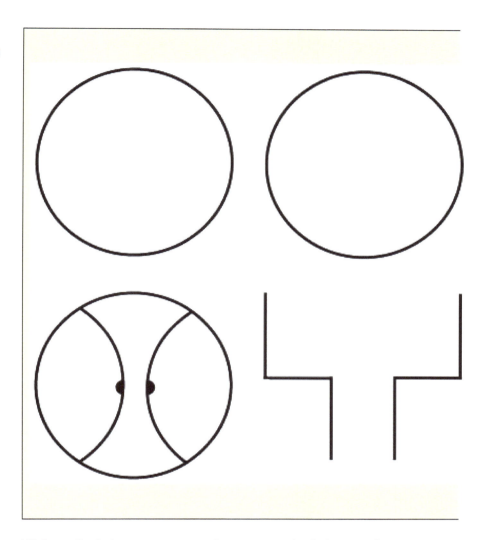

We've talked about our personal purpose and mission, our income goals and how to reach them, using the Wheel of Fortune for finding prospects, and how we set appointments to achieve success.

These symbols tell the story of how we make sales.

What do they mean to you?

*Face to Face*

*Belly to Belly*

*Knee to Knee*

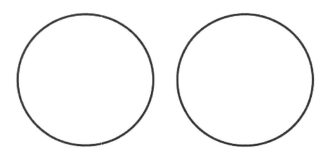

This represents face-to-face contact. Seeing people, in person, face-to-face, gives you a greater chance to make sales.

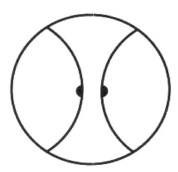

Get belly to belly with prospects means you'll learn what they need—and that will allow you to make sales.

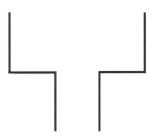

Being knee-to-knee means you're engaging your prospect, asking questions that will guide you to make a sale out of an appointment.

Your sales method is all about personal contact with prospects—getting face-to-face, belly-to-belly, and knee-to-knee.

That's the proven way to increase sales potential.

## Reducing or Eliminating Resistance

To reduce errors in communication:

> Use everyday vocabulary.

> Avoid using industry language, technical terms, and acronyms that only you would understand.

> Speak clearly.

> Let the Prospect set the pace of the conversation.

> Maintain good eye contact and smile.

> Pay close attention to the speaker.

> Pay attention to nonverbal signals.

> Focus on remembering what was said.

> Use questions and statements that affirm you are listening to the Prospect.

> Keep your emotions in check so as not to distort the message.

## Three Steps to Handling Objections

One of the biggest mistakes Sales Professionals make is to try and fight the Prospect's objections. When you fight an objection, your Prospect's sales resistance goes up and the sales process becomes much more difficult.

Instead of battling with your Prospect, align yourself with him or her and reinforce that you are on the Prospect's side. By aligning with your Prospect, you validate any concern which lowers sales resistance and makes objections much easier to overcome.

It is important to validate the Prospect's concerns because you want to:

- Demonstrate empathy.
- Acknowledge Prospect's feelings.
- Provide emotional concern.

Begin asking effective questions. It is important to begin asking effective questions to:

- Find out specifically what they don't like
- Find out specifically what they do like

Two things to remember when completing this step:

- Get permission to ask questions.
- Be polite.

The idea of answering objections is to:

- Provide enough information for the Prospect to make a buying decision TODAY.
- Rebuttals are designed to provide you with enough information to assist the Prospect in making a buying decision TODAY.

## *TYPICAL OBJECTIONS*

Objections? …. Buying signals? …. A need/request for "new" information to make a new decision?

1. Can you send me something in the mail?
2. I'm happy with my current [product/service/plan].
3. I never asked for any information or for any one to call me.
4. I really just want the bottom line … What's your [cost/price/minimum/best price be]?
5. I've got an [product/service/plan] now and like the way it works.
6. I've got [product/service/plan] … I was just look for some [product/service/plan].
7. I'm broke … you would just be wasting your time.

## REBUTTALS

1. ***Can you send me something in the mail****?*

**Salesperson Response**:

"Joe, thank goodness, you know enough about [product/service/plan] to ask a representative to do that for you. That tells me that you know a lot more about [product/service/plan] than the average person.

Did you know that you could now go on the Internet and look at all kinds of [product/service/plans]?

You can actually spend days looking at plans.

The only problem is that when you review these [product/service/plans] you still don't know what the [product/service/plan] will really do…

… You might know the [name a feature] and the [name a benefit] but it's not clear what the [product/service/plans] would do in regards to: [name four product/service/plan features/two product/service/plan benefits]

It's really sad now that companies and salespeople/representatives] will allow their clients to purchase [products/service/plans] that they don't understand or forgot to ASK! about something.
[Prospect's name], I'll tell you what I'll do … Now I Can't Do It TODAY

… I'm simply too busy …

Give me a couple of days to get it ready <u>SPECIFICALLY FOR YOU</u>
… but I've got in excess of [number of products/service/plans] over [number of options] different options that can be added to the [product/service/plans]

… but if you will give me a couple of days to prepare, I'll design a worksheet that will allow you to custom design your [product/service/plan] to meet the needs of your [business/company/team/family] and ensure you're getting the most for your money.

**Now**, [state prospects name] I see here that you are located [state address and city].

 I should have your information in a couple of days but I will not be in your area until [state day of week].

What time [state day] would be best for you to review the various options?"

2. ***I'm happy with my current [product/service/plan].***"

**Salesperson Response**:

 "It's refreshing to hear someone this day and time to say that they are happy with their [product/service/plan]. I strongly recommend that you keep that [product/service/plan] as long as possible.

[Prospects name], I notice here [state the number of years they have been in business/number of employees/industry they are in/state age].

This is a perfect time in [for the company/department/team/life to look at [ancillary product/service/plan].

[Prospects name], let me ask you something … If [your company/department/team] had a [typical product/service/plan costly problem] tomorrow, I know your [product/service/plan would do well and you were unable to [operate/service/market some part of their product/service/plan] would there be a lack of [benefit of your ancillary product/service/plan]?

… You know that you're at the perfect [business age/market condition/stage] to start looking at this type of [ancillary product/service/plan] …

At your [company/department/individual stage in business/volume/revenue] you can get a great deal [state ancillary product/service/plan for very little cost.

[Products/service/plans] like: [name three ancillary products/service plans/plans]
[state prospects name], since you already have your [product/service/plan] taken care of … it would not take me more than 15 minutes to let you review these options that would give yourself and your [company/department/team] a great deal of security.

I'll give you an example … for example a [give example of client who purchased ancillary product/service/plan …"

3. *I've never heard of your company.*

**Salesperson Response:**

"[prospects name] I don't know how active you are in the self-employed area … but [agency name here] Company has been around for 75 years and we have an A – Excellent Rating from AM Best.

We are one of the few companies in this state with that high of a rating.

While our plans are designed with benefits that the self-employed require such as on and off the job coverage, our coverage also can be very beneficial to those not self-employed but are still responsible for their own health insurance.

Understand that we have chosen to put our advertising dollars into keeping our costs down and enhancing benefits to our clients …

 As a result, most of my business comes from referrals."

4. *I've already met with one of your Salespersons.*

   **Salesperson Response:**

"That's Great [state prospects name]! …

When did you [contract/apply/enroll] to see if [you/your company/team] qualify for [state ancillary product/service/plan]?

You know [state prospects name] we have more than [state number of products/service plans/plans] and a lot of times an Salesperson just chooses a single [product/service plan/] plan to show a client

   … I've always found it to be more productive for me to spend a few hours in preparation before going to see a client and do an array of [product/service/plan] comparisons

   … in a very concise manner.

This allows the customer the COMFORT of being able to select the [product/service/plan] that most meets his needs and also ensures the customer the best value for their [PRODUCT/SERVICE/PLAN] DOLLARS.

While I would not step on someone's toes, it's obvious by the fact that you did not [contract/apply/enroll] to see if you would benefit … that you were not possibly given our full array of options.

[state your company name] is adamant that we work with our clients to ensure satisfaction ... I am not saying you have to make a final decision with me, but I'm going to be in your area on [state day of week]

... What time would be beneficial to sit down with you and your team?"

5. *I don't have time to meet with anyone ... I just need to get it handled*.

**Salesperson Response**:

"You and me BOTH! This company is running me ragged ... Tons of people to see and very little time to do it in before they give me another whole bunch of people who have called us.

I think its just the way the world is today.

Listen [state prospects name], I'll tell you what I'll do [see #1 above]"

6. *I don't want anything over [price/term/service agreement]*.

**Salesperson Response**:

"That's fine [state prospects name] ... I've got [products/service/plans] from [state range].

As a matter of fact, I'll even let you do combination [product/service/plans] if you would like. Like just [state example of combining your product/service/plan with an ancillary product/service/plan].
BUT ... ONE THING I'LL MAKE SURE YOU HAVE [state a product/service/plan feature that is one of your must have's!]"

**Now set the Appointment**

7. *I just want [product/service/plan]*.

**Salesperson Response**:

"If what you mean by [product/service/plan], I can do that, but I would encourage you to also make sure that things like: [unique product/service/plans/ancillary benefits you have] are also included on your [product/service/plan].

"I'll be glad to work up several options for us to review that will ensure your **SATISIFACTION** with the [product/service/plan/ we design."

## Sales Person Responses Quickview:

| | |
|---|---|
| "I've never heard of your company" | "That does not surprise me, the fact that we don't advertise is one of the very reasons we can save people money. There are over 1,000 companies in the U.S. providing [your product/service/plan]. We are one of the larger companies. Now, you are self-employed, aren't you? I can see you on [state day and time]. Will you be in then?" |
| "I'm not interested in buying [product/service/plan."<br><br>Or "I'm not interested." | "I wouldn't expect you to be interested in something you haven't even seen. That's why I'm calling for an appointment to show you how you can save money with an [your company name]. You are interested in saving money, aren't you?" "I can see you on [state day and time].<br>Will you be in then?" |
| "Just mail or leave informatic | "Well, [prospect name], we've already done that, and my job is to determine how you qualify and see if one of our [products/service/plans] may save you money. I can see you on [state day and time]. Will you be in then?" |
| "What does this cost?" | "We have several different [product/service/plans] available. That's why it's important for us to visit for a few minutes so that I can help you build a plan to fit your [company/team/personal] needs as well as your budget. I can see you [state day and time]. Will you be in then?" |
| "I'm [product/service/plan] poor.<br><br>Or I can't afford any more." | "Well, [prospect name], I know what you mean and I appreciate your Point of view, however there is a difference between [price/cost/rate] and [product/service/plan] and most small business owners find they can lower their [price/cost/rate]. I can see you on [state day and time]. Will you be in then?" |
| "I'm too busy right now" | "Well, [prospect name], I assumed you would be busy, that's why I phoned first. I will be in your area this week. What's the best time to call for an appointment? (If he continues to say he's too busy...) Well, you know you're never too busy to save money, are you? I can see you on [state day and time]. Will you be in then?" |
| "I'm not interested or I told that girl not to have anyone contact me" | "Well, you know [prospect name] that's exactly why I called today. 90% of the people that I've met with over the years were initially not interested, but what they found was that our investment of time together was actually valuable because we were able to either reduce their out of [price/costs/rate] or increase their benefits... and in some cases, we accomplished both. With your permission, I would like to offer that same service to you. I can see you on [state day and time]. Will you be in then?" |

**Timeless Closes**

There really is nothing new when it comes to training sales people or learning sales processes. Dale Carnegie wrote a book in 1936 "How To Win Friends and Influence People", it has been the bible for salespeople for many years, not much has changed.

As a treat, I am including here some of the best closes that have ever been used, some are done with a legal pad, some with a white board, most use the old adage to think in ink, these closes demonstrate the best example of these timeless closes. Enjoy!

**Lifetime Close**

"During our lifetime, we buy many things –

cars, televisions, homes, etc.

And always before investing our money, we consider three things:

 Do I need it?  Do I like it?  Can I afford it? (Cost)

"Regardless what you buy you accept or reject a purchase based on asking yourself these three questions, right?

Now let's look at the [product/service/plan] you designed;

- Do you like the [product/service/plan] you designed?
- Do you feel you and your [business/company/team/family] need this?
- Do you feel comfortable with the company?
- Can you handle the cost?

"The only time you can apply for this [product/service/plan] is when you are in good [financial/market/competitive]; position to take advantage of it.

Let's authorize [your company] to run a clearance and get a [delivery/start/credit approval] so you can start [picking up lost sales/increase revenue/reduce cost]?"

## Want to Shop Around Close

"Obviously, you have a reason for feeling this way, do you mind if I ask what it is?"
- "Tell me a little bit about what you are shopping around for so I can give you some information to help you make an informed and intelligent decision"
- "Let's start the [approval/contracting/service] process to protect your ability to qualify while you still have a choice to shop around"

## No Money Close

"Obviously, you have a reason for feeling this way, do you mind if I ask what it is?"

"Suppose you needed a new job. You walk into one place of business and are offered your current salary with no health benefits.

When you get sick or hurt, or a member of your family goes to the hospital, your employer will not be able to pay anything towards your medical bills.

That's what your current job is now, isn't it?

Then, suppose you walked down the street and talked to another employer who offered a job which had the same hours and duties.

He said he would pay you (state cost) less than what you are currently getting.

However, he would pay you (list the policy benefits discussed).

Which job would you take?

Why?

This is exactly the choice you have now and it is the choice you can make only when you are in good financial health.

Let's authorize the company to check your history to see what you qualify for."

## Talk to Spouse Close

- "Obviously, you have a reason for feeling this way, do you mind if I ask what it is?"
- Call the spouse
- Go to where the spouse is
- Get the spouse info and then schedule
- Deal with this up front prior to setting the appointment

**No Need Close**

"Let's look at it this way:

Let's weigh your obligation against our obligation:

(Write cost of product/service/plan)    (List product/service/plan benefits)

First of all, your obligation is to set aside (state cost here).

On the other hand, our obligation is to [pay/service/protect/provide] you:

[List all the benefits you are recommending in the "our" column]

However, if you do not live up to your obligation and set aside [state cost here], then our obligation becomes yours (put "Y" in front of "our") and you have to meet these [expenses/service/provide] as well as your other regular expenses.

Certainly, the wisest decision here is to set aside (state cost) and let [your company] help [pay/service/protect/provide] these [your features/benefits] for you.

Your business health is your wealth and you can only make this decision while you are in good business health.

Let's authorize [your company] run a clearance if get you qualified."

**No Hurry Close**

"If this were a purchase of a product where a few days wouldn't matter, I'd say fine, however, let me point out that [features/benefits of your product/service/plans] of this kind is never on sale.

In other words… it will never be any cheaper.

As a matter of fact, it will be more expensive and could possibly "go off the market" as far as your credit/business/market health is concerned.

Today it looks like you are in good credit/business/market health, but before tomorrow can fail. When you wait one day, you may be one of the persons who cannot qualify.

Remember, Mr. _____, you take the chance but when you lose, your company/business/team/family] pays.

Let's move on this now while you are in good credit/business/market health."

**Price is too high Close**

"Obviously, you have a reason for feeling this way, do you mind if I ask what it is?"

- "Let's look at the features – which one can your [business/team/family] do without?"
- "Is it more than you are willing to pay or is this [product/service/plan more than you expected?"
- "What range did you want to stay in?"

**Don't have a better [product/service/plan] Close**

"Obviously, you have a reason for feeling that way, do you mind if I ask what it is?"

- "What are the features of your [product/service/plan] that you have used the most?"
- "If we do, are there any issues that would prevent you from qualifying?
- "That's a good idea, lets look at it and see"

**Thinking it over Close**

"Obviously, you have a reason for feeling that way, do you mind if I ask what it is?"

- "Specifically, what are you going to think about, the features, the benefits or the cost?"
- "There are two decisions to make, first the [Corp office/accounting/manager] has to make a decision that they are willing to accept your company credit/market/industry health as a risk, etc"

**Better price with Close**

"Obviously, you have a reason for feeling that way, do you mind if I ask what it is?"
- "What features does that price include?"
- "What is the price you feel you can get?"
- "Do you mind if I ask why I am here, in other words is there a specific reason you did not take that policy?

# CHAPTER 6 - LEAD TYPES AND STRATEGIES

**Type of Piece:**   **Referral Lead**

<u>Description:</u>   This is by far the best lead you can have.  The salesperson generates it by speaking with prospects or policyholders.  It can occur whether or not a sale is made to the original prospect.

<u>When Received:</u>  Any time you speak to a prospect, there is an opportunity to receive referral leads.  Most salespeople fail to generate this type of lead, for three reasons: One – they simply don't ask.
Two – they do not have the proper mind set.  It is important that a salesperson understands that this is part of the sales process.  People want to help, and if asked properly, they will.
Three – Salespeople aren't sure what to say or do.  It is important that you ask for the names of at least 50 people the prospect could introduce you to.  When asked for such a large number of names, the prospect often gives nine or ten contacts.  If you ask for only one name, you will probably get no one!  Suggest the prospect get out their address book.  You should have a list, numbered 1-50, so the prospect knows you are serious.  When the prospect offers the first name and telephone number, it's important to write that by number 50, NOT number 1.  The prospect will feel they must fill in the other lines.  TRY THIS – IT WORKS!

<u>Why Generated:</u>  Referrals are generated because a prospect has recognized that some of their friends and neighbors have needs that they believe your products can meet, and they trust you to provide the information.

<u>How Do You Approach:</u>  Again, this is a person who has been introduced to you by someone they respect; they have confidence that the person who introduced you has been happy with your services?  Usually, the referral and the original prospect have similar needs and interests. (Remember – <u>Birds of a feather flock together</u>!)  People are always interested in making sure they are current on their coverage; they easily grant appointments for coverage review.  Most prospects are not paying too much for their insurance, but are paying too much for what they have.  Professionals program their insurance needs and doesn't just "sell a policy."

<u>When Do You Work the Lead:</u>  These should be worked as soon as possible.  It is very disturbing to both the person who is referring and to their friends and neighbors if a salesperson receives permission to call and doesn't follow up promptly.

<u>Product:</u>   This is not a product-specific lead.  It is intended as a fact-finding mission.  The review can uncover many needs.

<u>What Do You Say:</u>  "Mrs. Jones, I am calling because I was able to help a friend of yours, (Name), with his/her insurance coverage.  I may be able to help you by reviewing your

coverage and answering some questions that you may have.  I will be in your area on (Date).  Would (3:00 or 4:00) be better for you?"

**Type of Piece:**    **Company/carrier Lead**

Description:    This is a card generated by your company/agency/carrier to request product information, a price comparison, coverage review, etc.

When Received:    faxes Home Office leads as they become available to agency managers.

Why Generated:    Company/agency/carrier Leads are created because a prospect or policyholder contacts the Home Office to request product information, a price comparison, coverage review, etc.

How Do You Approach:    The person you are approaching has expressed an interest in at least one product, or has asked for a coverage review. Because they are interested, they easily grant appointments for coverage review.

When Do You Work the Lead:    These prospects are eager to have you take care of their needs.  It is critical that you contact them as soon as possible!

Product:    This lead is intended as a fact-finding mission.  Contact the prospect first about their expressed interest.  The review can uncover other needs.  Many times, by asking about the prospect's needs relating to other products, you can get additional sales.  (For example, you may create an interest in Long Term Care insurance by asking what the prospect has done to protect them from financial disaster resulting from a stay in a nursing home.)

What Do You Say:    "Mrs. Jones, I am calling because you contacted [Agency name] and expressed an interest in (product.)  I will be in your area on (Date).  Would (3:00 or 4:00) be better for you?"

Type of Piece:   **E-commerce Lead**

Description:   This is a card generated by an internet lead vendor to request product information, a price comparison, coverage review, etc.

When Received:   faxes Home Office leads as they become available to agency managers.

Why Generated:   American Eagle Earned Leads are created because a prospect or policyholder visits the American Eagle web site and requests product information, a price comparison, coverage review, etc.

How Do You Approach:   The person you are approaching has expressed an interest in at least one product, or has asked for a coverage review.  Because they are interested, they easily grant appointments for coverage review.

When Do You Work the Lead:   These prospects are eager to have you take care of their needs.  It is critical that you contact them as soon as possible!

Product:   This lead is intended as a fact-finding mission.  Contact the prospect first about their expressed interest.  The review can uncover other needs.  Many times, by asking about the prospect's needs relating to other products, you can get additional sales.  (For example, you may create an interest in Long Term Care insurance by asking what the prospect has done to protect themselves from financial disaster resulting from a stay in a nursing home.)

What Do You Say:   This lead was generated through the Internet, so there may not be a telephone number provided.  You may need to send an introductory email before setting a face-to-face appointment.

Type of Piece:   **Anniversary Lead**

Description:    Anniversary Leads are current policyholders. They have an active salesperson. Vital information (e.g., name, address, telephone number) is included on the card.  For the most part, this information is correct; however, people's situations change – they move, change telephone numbers, etc.

When Received:  Anniversary Leads are routinely provided monthly to agency managers.  They are sent prior to the policyholder's coverage anniversary.  (For example, policyholders with an anniversary date in March would be sent during the first half of February.)  An agency manager may also request Anniversary Leads.

Why Generated:  A policy anniversary is a natural occasion to review the policyholder's coverage.  Because the needs of prospects often change, through death, inheritance, illness, etc., a review of coverage using the fact finder often opens the door for further sales.

How Do You Approach:  The person you are approaching has already bought at least one product from us.  They are interested in making sure they are current on their coverage, and easily grant appointments for coverage review.

When Do You Work the Lead:  These are best worked prior to the policy anniversary, it works well to combine them with other sales activities in an area.  You could drop by on some Anniversary Leads if you have another appointment that is cancelled.  You should always have some Anniversary Leads with you when you go on sales calls.

Product:    This lead is intended as a fact-finding mission. The review can uncover other needs.  Many times, by asking about the prospect's needs relating to other products, you can get additional sales.  (For example, you may create an interest in Long-Term Care insurance by asking what the prospect has done to protect them from financial disaster resulting from a stay in a nursing home.)

What Do You Say:  "Mrs. Jones, I am calling to provide the annual review of your coverage with us, to let you know of any changes in your coverage and to answer questions you may have.  I will be in your area on (Date).  Would (3:00 or 4:00) be better for you?"

Type of Piece:   **Orphan Lead**

Description:      Orphan Leads are current policyholders, but the salesperson who wrote the policy is no longer servicing them. Vital information (e.g., name, address, telephone number) is included on the card. For the most part, this information is correct; however, people's situations change – they move, change telephone numbers, etc.

When Received:  Orphan Leads are routinely provided monthly to agency managers. They are sent prior to the policyholder's coverage anniversary. (For example, policyholders with an anniversary date in March would be sent during the first half of February.) An agency manager may also request Anniversary Leads.

Why Generated:  A policy anniversary is a natural occasion to review the policyholder's coverage. Because the needs of prospects often change, through death, inheritance, illness, etc., a review of coverage using the fact finder often opens the door for further sales.

How Do You Approach:  The person you are approaching has already bought at least one product from us. They are interested in making sure they are current on their coverage, and easily grant appointments for coverage review.

When Do You Work the Lead:  These are best worked prior to the policy anniversary. It works well to combine them with other sales activities in an area. You could drop by on some Orphan Leads if you have another appointment that is cancelled. You should always have some Orphan Leads with you when you go on sales calls.

Product:         This lead is intended as a fact-finding mission. The review can uncover other needs. Many times, by asking about the prospect's needs relating to other products, you can get additional sales. (For example, you may create an interest in Long-Term Care insurance by asking what the prospect has done to protect them from financial disaster resulting from a stay in a nursing home.)

What Do You Say:  "Mrs. Jones, I am calling to provide the annual review of your coverage with us, to let you know of any changes in your coverage and to answer questions you may have. I will be in your area on (Date). Would (3:00 or 4:00) be better for you?"

**Type of Piece:** **Medicare Supplement Direct Mail**

**Description:** This is a mailer for Medicare supplement insurance that a prospect has returned, indicating they are interested in information on the product. However, sometimes the prospect is interested in other products.

**When Received:** Direct Mail responses are sent to you weekly by the vendor providers. Responses begin approximately three weeks after the mailers are sent to prospects; it takes about seven to 10 days from the time a prospect mails a responder card until the salesperson receives the card.

**Why Generated:** Direct Mail responses occur because prospects react to a mailer for a specific product – in this case, Medicare supplement insurance.

**How Do You Approach:** The person you are approaching has shown an interest in Medicare supplement. The mailer card may include such information as date of birth and telephone number. BE CAREFUL! Sometimes the person to whom the card was mailed did not send in the response; a spouse, son or daughter may have returned the card.

**When Do You Work the Lead:** Direct Mail leads do NOT get better with age; they should be worked thoroughly as soon as possible.

**Product:** You should always start with the product the mailer was directed toward, in this case, Medicare supplement. However, by asking about the prospect's needs relating to other products, you may get additional sales. (For example, you may create an interest in Long Term Care insurance by asking what the prospect has done to protect them from financial disaster resulting from a stay in a nursing home.)

**What Do You Say:** "Mrs. Jones, you recently indicated an interest in Medicare supplement insurance, as I understand by the card you returned to our company. I will be in your area on (Date). Would (3:00 or 4:00) be better for you?"

**Message: 2016 Medicare Health Plan Update**

*2016 Healthcare Plan Update*

You may not be getting all the Medicare benefits for which you are eligible. There are new plans for 2016 that you should be aware of.

**You may be missing out on what you are eligible to receive.**

Complete and return the attached postage free card to find out if you currently receive all the benefits you are eligible for.

There is no obligation and all the information is FREE!

B-KK12

No cost or obligation. Not affiliated with any government agency. A representative may call. This solicitation is insurance related.

Type of Piece:  **Medicare Supplement/Long-Term Care Combination Direct Mail**

Description:     This is a mailer for both Medicare supplement insurance and/or Long-Term Care insurance that a prospect has returned, indicating they are interested in information on one or more of the products.  However, sometimes the prospect is interested in other products.

When Received:  Direct Mail responses are sent to you weekly by vendor providers.  Responses begin approximately three weeks after the mailers are sent to prospects; it takes about seven to 10 days from the time a prospect mails a responder card until the salesperson receives the card.

Why Generated:  Direct Mail responses occur because prospects react to a mailer for a specific product – in this case, Medicare supplement insurance and/or Long Term Care insurance.

How Do You Approach:  The person you are approaching has shown an interest in Medicare supplement and/or Long-Term Care.  The mailer card may include such information as date of birth and telephone number.  BE CAREFUL!  Sometimes the person to whom the card was mailed did not send in the response; a spouse, son or daughter may have returned the card.
Be sure you are ready to go from either Long-Term Care to Medicare supplement or from Medicare supplement to Long-Term Care in your approach.  The prospect may be more interested in one product than in the other, or they may be interested in both.

When Do You Work the Lead:  Direct Mail leads do NOT get better with age; they should be worked thoroughly as soon as possible.

Product:        You should always start with the product the mailer was directed toward, in this case, Medicare supplement and/or Long Term Care.  However, by asking about the prospect's needs relating to other products, you may get additional sales. (For example, if they are interested in Long Term Care, you should find out if you can save them money on their current Medicare supplement coverage.)

What Do You Say:  "Mrs. Jones, you recently indicated an interest in (Medicare supplement) (Long Term Care) insurance, as I understand by the card you returned to our company. I will be in your area on (Date).  Would (3:00 or 4:00) be better for you?"

**Type of Piece:**     **Long-Term Care Direct Mail**

Description:     This is a mailer for Long-Term Care insurance that a prospect has returned, indicating they are interested in information on the product. However, sometimes the prospect is interested in other products.

When Received:  Direct Mail responses are sent to you weekly by vendor providers. Responses begin approximately three weeks after the mailers are sent to prospects; it takes about seven to 10 days from the time a prospect mails a responder card until the salesperson receives the card.

Why Generated:  Direct Mail responses occur because prospects react to a mailer for a specific product – in this case, Long Term Care insurance.

How Do You Approach:  The person you are approaching has shown an interest in Long-Term Care. The mailer card may include such information as date of birth and telephone number. BE CAREFUL! Sometimes the person to whom the card was mailed did not send in the response; a spouse, son or daughter may have returned the card.

When Do You Work the Lead:  Direct Mail leads do NOT get better with age; they should be worked thoroughly as soon as possible.

Product:     You should always start with the product the mailer was directed toward, in this case, Long Term Care. However, by asking about the prospect's needs relating to other products, you may get additional sales. (For example, you should find out if you can save them money on their current Medicare supplement coverage.)

What Do You Say:  "Mrs. Jones, you recently indicated an interest in Long-Term Care insurance, as I understand by the card you returned to our company. I will be in your area on (Date). Would (3:00 or 4:00) be better for you?"

# CHANGES IN YOUR MEDICARE BENEFITS

As of January 1st, many Medicare Supplement insurers have increased their rates up to 30% in the last two years on Medicare supplement coverage.

Based on this, there is now available a plan in your state to supplement Medicare at lower rates for residents over 65 years of age.

You must detach and mail the attached postage-paid card to receive this vital information. This latest information is being held until you request it. Please verify that your address is correct on the attached card and please…

MAIL TODAY TO RECEIVE THIS VITAL INFORMATION…
REQUESTS WILL BE PROCESSED IN THE ORDER RECEIVED…
REQUESTS RETURNED MORE THAN 15 DAYS FROM RECEIPT OF THIS
NOTICE MAY NOT BE PROCESSED

B-AM9

**Type of Piece:**   **Annuity Direct Mail**

**Description:**   This is a mailer for annuities that a prospect has returned, indicating they are interested in information on the product. The mailer referenced such things as tax advantages, probate, interest rates, etc. However, sometimes the prospect is interested in other products.

**When Received:**   Direct Mail responses are sent to you weekly by vendor providers. Responses begin approximately three weeks after the mailers are sent to prospects; it takes about seven to 10 days from the time a prospect mails a responder card until the salesperson receives the card.

**Why Generated:**   Direct Mail responses occur because prospects react to a mailer for a specific product – in this case, annuities.

**How Do You Approach:**   The person you are approaching has shown an interest in annuities. The mailer card may include such information as date of birth and telephone number. BE CAREFUL! Sometimes the person to whom the card was mailed <u>did not</u> send in the response; a spouse, son or daughter may have returned the card.

**When Do You Work the Lead:**   Direct Mail leads do NOT get better with age; they should be worked thoroughly as soon as possible.

**Product:**   You should always start with the product the mailer was directed toward, in this case, annuities. However, by asking about the prospect's needs relating to other products, you may get additional sales. (For example, you may create an interest in Long-Term Care insurance by asking what the prospect has done to protect themselves from financial disaster resulting from a stay in a nursing home.) People who return annuity mailers usually have assets to protect. This is an excellent reason to mention Long Term Care insurance and asset protection.

**What Do You Say:**   "Mrs. Jones, you recently indicated an interest in our financial products and what they can do for you, as I understand by the card you returned to our company. I will be in your area on (Date). Would (3:00 or 4:00) be better for you?"

Type of Piece:    **Final Expense Life Direct Mail**

Description:    This is a mailer for Final Expense life insurance that a prospect has returned, indicating they are interested in information on the product. However, sometimes the prospect is interested in other products.

When Received:    Direct Mail responses are sent to you weekly by vendor providers. Responses begin approximately three weeks after the mailers are sent to prospects; it takes about seven to 10 days from the time a prospect mails a responder card until the salesperson receives the card.

Why Generated:    Direct Mail responses occur because prospects react to a mailer for a specific product – in this case, Final Expense life insurance.

How Do You Approach:    The person you are approaching has shown an interest in Final Expense Life. The mailer card may include such information as date of birth and telephone number. BE CAREFUL! Sometimes the person to whom the card was mailed did not send in the response; a spouse, son or daughter may have returned the card.

When Do You Work the Lead:    Direct Mail leads do NOT get better with age; they should be worked thoroughly as soon as possible.

Product:    You should always start with the product the mailer was directed toward, in this case, Final Expense life. However, by asking about the prospect's needs relating to other products, you may get additional sales. (For example, you may create an interest in Long Term Care insurance by asking what the prospect has done to protect themselves from financial disaster resulting from a stay in a nursing home. You should also find out if you could save them money on their current Medicare supplement coverage.)

What Do You Say:    "Mrs. Jones, you recently indicated an interest in Final Expense life insurance, as I understand by the card you returned to our company. I will be in your area on (Date). Would (3:00 or 4:00) be better for you?"

Or, "Mrs. Jones, you recently returned a card to us, indicating your interest in coverage to help pay for funeral and burial expenses. I will be in your area on (Date). Would (3:00 or 4:00) be better for you?"

---

### New 2015 Benefit Update for &lt;State&gt; Citizens

This is a personal announcement to all &lt;State&gt; citizens age 50-85.

You may now apply for a NEW state-regulated life insurance program to pay Final Expenses for just pennies a day, REGARDLESS OF YOUR MEDICAL CONDITION, EVEN IF YOU'VE BEEN TURNED DOWN BEFORE.

Return this card today and you will receive the latest information on how this Special Program will pay 100% of all funeral expenses not paid by government funds, up to $25,000 (**TAX FREE**), for each &lt;State&gt; citizen covered.

It is VERY IMPORTANT THAT YOU KNOW all the benefits available to you. To receive complete NO-COST information on this newly-approved plan ***DESIGNED FOR ALL &lt;STATE&gt; CITIZENS***, return this postage paid card TODAY.

*TO SEE IF YOU QUALIFY, COMPLETE THIS POSTAGE PAID CARD TODAY TO RECEIVE THIS VITAL INFORMATION... REQUESTS WILL BE PROCESSED IN THE ORDER RECEIVED.*

**Type of Piece:** **Late Responder List**

**Description:** This is a list of names, addresses and (when possible) telephone numbers of prospects that have recently received a direct mailer form. For the most part, they have not yet returned the mailers.

**When Received:** Late responder lists are generated each time a direct mailing is done. Vendor providers send the late responder lists, on a CD or email attachment, two - four weeks after the mailing is sent. You should receive the Late Responder list for a mailing about the same time they receive the first response cards from the mailing.

**Why Generated:** Direct mail prospects often are interested in the products offered, but they forget to return the card, or they misplace or accidentally destroy the card. Sometimes their circumstances change after they receive the mailing, and they have a need that did not exist when they first received the response card. When a salesperson contacts them, these prospects often remember receiving the mailer, and may be quite interested.

**How Do You Approach:** The person you are approaching has received a mailer for one of your products. Which product the mailer was designed for will determine how you approach the prospects. Salespeople should keep the product and the criteria for that product in mind when contacting people on a late responder list. (If you are unsure, please ask your manager for the focus of the mailer for the list you are working from.) It is important for salespeople to cluster their direct response leads with late responders in order to maximize their sales efforts. Late responders can be organized by zip code by your manager to provide the clustering effect – you could receive two direct mail responses in a zip code and also call on six or eight late responders in the same zip code.

**When Do You Work the Lead:** Direct Mail leads do NOT get better with age; they should be worked thoroughly as soon as possible. Since late responders are worked concurrently with direct mail leads, late responders should also be worked promptly.

**Product:** You should always start with the product the mailer was directed toward, whether it is Medicare supplement, Long-Term Care, annuities or Final Expense Life. However, by asking about the prospect's needs relating to other products, you may get additional sales.

**What Do You Say:** "Mrs. Jones, I'm calling because we recently sent you a mailer about (Product). I'm sure you have some questions about this type of coverage. We may be able to help you; I will be in your area on (Date) to review this with you. Would (3:00 or 4:00) be better for you?"

Type of Piece:    **Telemarketed Lead**

Description:    This is a card that is generated by professional telemarketers, working for an outside vendor that is contracted to provide lead generation.

When Received:  Telemarketed leads are sent weekly or daily, depending on the service you purchased from affiliate vendor providers.

Why Generated:  Telemarketed leads are designed to offer a specific product to prospects within a specific area.

How Do You Approach:  The person you are approaching has had a telephone conversation with the telemarketer, and has indicated that they have an interest in this particular product (usually Medicare supplement.)  Be aware that many times spouse requests information for their partner, and the person you speak to may not be the same person who spoke with the telemarketer.

When Do You Work the Lead:  Telemarketed leads DO NOT get better with age.  They should be worked thoroughly as soon as possible.  The longer the wait, the less likely the prospect will remember the telephone call.

Product:    You should always start with the product the person has expressed interest in (for telemarketed leads, usually Medicare supplement or Long-Term Care.  However, by asking about the prospect's needs relating to other products, you may get additional sales.  (For example, you may create an interest in Long-Term Care insurance by asking what the prospect has done to protect them from financial disaster resulting from a stay in a nursing home.)

What Do You Say:  "Mrs. Jones, you recently expressed an interest in Medicare supplement insurance, as I understand by a telephone conversation you had with a member of our organization.  I will be in your area on (Date) to review this with you.  Would (3:00 or 4:00) be better for you?"

Type of Piece:   **Profile Leads**

Description:   These are cards with names, addresses and telephone numbers of prospects who are age 75 to 80.  They have NOT been contacted, either by telephone or through the mail.

When Received:  Profile Leads are mailed weekly to you by Vendor providers.

Why Generated:  These are prospects who may be interested in one or more products, but who might not be approached by a salesperson.  When contacted, they may be very interested.  The intent of profile leads is to provide salespeople additional prospects in a zip code where they are already receiving leads of other types.  Profile leads should be clustered with direct mail leads, tele-leads, orphans or other leads.

How Do You Approach:  The person you are approaching has not been contacted prior to your call or visit; however, they are likely to share similar needs with other prospects, and may be willing to set an appointment for coverage review.

When Do You Work the Lead:  It works well to combine Profile leads with other sales activities in an area.  You could drop by on some Profile Leads if you have another appointment that is cancelled.  You should always have some Profile Leads with you when you go on sales calls.

Product:   You should always begin with a thought-provoking idea. Concepts regarding changes in Medicare, etc., often create interest.  As prospects, these prospects are concerned about Long-Term Care, Final Expense Life, etc.  However, events may trigger the use of other products.

What Do You Say:  "Mrs. Jones, I'm calling because Medicare recently had some changes in benefits that may affect you.  I know you have some questions about this.  I'm sure we can respond to your questions and concerns.  I will be in your area on (Date) to review this with you.  Would (3:00 or 4:00) be better for you?"

Type of Piece:  **Hot Leads**

Description:  Hot Leads are generated from vendors prospecting database.  These people previously responded either to a direct mail piece or to a telemarketing call.  A salesperson contacted them at least 90 days prior, and provided the information from that contact to the Home Office.  The prospect's circumstances may have changed since then, creating a new or more urgent need.

When Received:  Hot Leads are mailed on cards weekly to you by vendor providers. Although the leads are fresh, the information may or may not be the same as when it was gathered.

Why Generated:  Prospects' needs change all the time.  If approached again, a prospect that had little interest at first may be more approachable now.  Many veteran salespeople prefer these leads. They feel that the original salesperson established the contact and introduced the prospect to the product; an experienced veteran, with good telephone skills, often is successful in setting an appointment and discovering the needs of these prospects.

How Do You Approach:  The lead will give you the product for which it was generated, you should contact these prospects with that in mind.  If not sure, please ask your manager for the lead's purpose.

When Do You Work the Lead:  It works well to combine Hot Leads with other sales activities in a defined area.

Product:  You should always begin with the product for which the lead was originally created.  However, events may trigger the use of other products.

What Do You Say:  "Mrs. Jones, I'm calling because you previously indicated you had an interest in (Product).  Your needs may have changed since we spoke with you last.  I will be in your area on (Date) to review this with you.  Would (3:00 or 4:00) be better for you?"

---

**Message: 2016 Medicare Health Plan Update**

*2016 Healthcare Plan Update*

You may not be getting all the Medicare benefits for which you are eligible. There are new plans for 2016 that you should be aware of.

### You may be missing out on what you are eligible to receive.

Complete and return the attached postage free card to find out if you currently receive all the benefits you are eligible for.

There is no obligation and all the information is FREE!

B-KK12

*No cost or obligation. Not affiliated with any government agency. A representative may call. This solicitation is insurance related.*

Type of Piece:   **Database Lead**

Description:   These are generated from vendor providers prospecting database.  These people previously responded either to a direct mail piece or to a telemarketing call.  A salesperson contacted them and provided information to the Home Office.  The commonality among them is usually their current health insurance carrier.

When Received:  Database leads are mailed either as lists or on cards at the request of an agency manager.   Although the leads are fresh, the information may or may not be the same as when it was gathered.

Why Generated:  An agency manager requests Database leads because of a certain event, such as a large rate increase by a competitor (e.g., Blue Cross Blue Shield) or an HMO breaking up or a carrier pulling out of a state.  Database leads are clusters of prospects that are insured with the carrier involved in the event.  This gives salespeople an opportunity to offer these prospects an option to their current coverage.

How Do You Approach:  The lead will give you the criteria (the name of the competing insurer) for which it was generated.  You should contact these prospects with the current event in mind.  If not sure, please ask your manager for the lead's purpose.

When Do You Work the Lead:  These events have a very short window of opportunity.  It is important that they be worked as quickly as possible.

Product:   Medicare Supplement is usually the product.  However, events may trigger the use of other products.

What Do You Say:  "Mrs. Jones, I'm calling because (describe event.)  The last time we spoke with you, (competitor) was your carrier.  I'm sure you would like to consider what your other options are.   I will be in your area on (Date).  Would (3:00 or 4:00) be better for you?"

Type of Piece:  **Turning 65 Cards**

Description:  These are cards with the names, addresses and telephone numbers of people who are within six months of the month of their 65th birthday.

When Received:  These leads are sent on 3" x 5" cards to you by the vendor.  The list is also available on CD or email.  Usually, each shipment of cards covers a six-month period.

Why Generated:  Ninety-five percent of all prospects buy a Medicare supplement policy within six months of their 65th birthday, because of Medicare's open enrollment during this time.

How Do You Approach:  These are people are turning 65 years old, they will sign up for social security, automatically be enrolled in Medicare and 80% will buy a supplement.

When Do You Work the Lead:  Any time the prospect is with six months of their 65th birthday, up to the month they actually turn 65.  Medicare supplement policies may be written up to six months prior to the applicant's birthday, with coverage not starting until they go on Medicare (the first day of the month they turn 65.) PLEASE NOTE:  People who turn 65 on the first day of the month start on Medicare the first day of the previous month.

Product:  Medicare supplement is usually the product.  However, these people may be retiring and may lose their life insurance benefits from their employer.  Also, they may need an annuity to roll over their retirement benefits from work.  They may also need an immediate annuity to create an income stream.  Long-Term Care insurance is another possibility.  Many salespeople go for the Medicare supplement and fail to recognize and respond to the other insurance needs of the prospect.  If we don't meet their needs, the competition WILL!

Don't forget, these people are accustomed to paying a considerable amount for their health care, even if they had coverage through their employer.  This means that after retirement, after satisfying multiple needs, they may be paying less money than they had been before retirement.

What Do You Say:  "Mrs. Jones, I see you are turning 65 in (month.)  Like most people, you probably have questions about Medicare.  I will be in your area on (Date). Would (3:00 or 4:00) be better for you?"

### CHANGES IN YOUR MEDICARE BENEFITS

As of January 1st, many Medicare Supplement insurers have increased their rates up to 30% in the last two years on Medicare supplement coverage.

Based on this, there is now available a plan in your state to supplement Medicare at lower rates for residents over 65 years of age.

You must detach and mail the attached postage-paid card to receive this vital information. This latest information is being held until you request it. Please verify that your address is correct on the attached card and please...

MAIL TODAY TO RECEIVE THIS VITAL INFORMATION...
REQUESTS WILL BE PROCESSED IN THE ORDER RECEIVED...REQUESTS
RETURNED MORE THAN 15 DAYS FROM RECEIPT OF THIS NOTICE
MAY NOT BE PROCESSED

**Type of Piece:** **Turning 70 Cards**

**Description:** These are cards with the names, addresses and telephone numbers of people who are within six months of the month of their 70th birthday.

**When Received:** These are sent on 3" x 5" cards to you by the vendor. The list is also available on CD or email. Usually, each shipment of cards covers a six-month period.

**Why Generated:** Because most people buy Medicare supplement when they turn 65 years old, the anniversary of that policy is the month of their birthday. In many cases, they receive a very large rate increase when they turn 70, because they now fall into a different rate bracket. Furthermore, often these people have not seen a salesperson or reviewed their coverage since they bought their Medicare supplement five years previously. Also, because Long Term Care and life products are rated by age, they can still purchase these before their 70th birthday, to save money.

**How Do You Approach:** Many times a birthday letter, including our rates for Medicare supplement (with the appropriate rates highlighted) is sent in advance of a telephone call or personal call. This often makes the approach easier.

**When Do You Work the Lead:** The best time is about 30 to 45 days prior to the first day of the month in which their birthday falls. Many insurance companies send out premium notices 45 days ahead of the due date because they know prospects often pay a bill as soon as they receive it. They also know other insurance companies' salespeople will be contacting the prospects around their birthday. But if the senior has already paid the premium, (s)he is unlikely to replace the policy, unless payment is set up as a monthly bank draft. Remember that the policy probably went in force on the first day of the month they turned 65, so the renewal date is the first day of the month of their birthday.

**Product:** Medicare supplement is usually the product. However, if they are happy with their present coverage, you should pivot to Long-Term Care or Final Expense Life. Also, many prospects have not started taking distributions from their qualified retirement plans (such as IRAs.) They are required to take at least minimum distribution at age 70 ½. If they do not, they must pay a 50% penalty on the amount they should have taken and pay Federal income tax on that amount.

**What Do You Say:** "Mrs. Jones, I see you have a birthday coming up in (month.) Like many people, you have or will be getting a rate increase on your Medicare supplement. Also, there may be some changes in your retirement plans. In addition to possibly offering you more benefits, we may be able to save you some money. I will be in your area on (Date). Would (3:00 or 4:00) be better for you?"

Type of Piece:     **Turning 66 through 69 Cards**

Description:     These are cards with the names, addresses and telephone numbers of people who are within six months of the month of their 66th, 67th, 68th or 69th birthday.

When Received:  This list is sent on 3" x 5" cards to you by the vendor. The list is also available on CD or email. Usually, each shipment of cards covers a six-month period.

Why Generated:  Because most people buy Medicare supplement when they turn 65 years old, the anniversary of that policy is the month of their birthday. It is likely that they will have a premium increase due to their new age, and changes occur in Medicare each year. Also, because Long-Term Care and life products are rated by age, they can still purchase these before their next birthday, to save money.

How Do You Approach:  Many times a birthday letter, including our rates for Medicare supplement (with the appropriate rates highlighted) is sent in advance of a telephone call or personal call. This often makes the approach easier.

When Do You Work the Lead:  The best time is about 30 to 45 days prior to the first day of the month in which their birthday falls. Many insurance companies send out premium notices 45 days ahead of the due date because they know prospects often pay a bill as soon as they receive it. They also know other insurance companies' salespeople will be contacting the prospects around their birthday. But if the senior has already paid the premium, (s) he is unlikely to replace the policy, unless payment is set up as a monthly bank draft. Remember that the policy probably went in force on the first day of the month they turned 65, so the renewal date is the first day of the month of their birthday.

Product:     Medicare supplement is usually the product. However, if they are happy with their present coverage, you should pivot to Long-Term Care or Final Expense Life.

What Do You Say:  "Mrs. Jones, I see you have a birthday coming up in (month). Like many people, you have or will be getting a rate increase on your Medicare supplement. In addition to possibly offering you more benefits, we may be able to save you some money. I will be in your area on (Date). Would (3:00 or 4:00) be better for you?"

---

MEDICARE OPEN ENROLLMENT INQUIRY CARD

When you turn age 65, you will be in your Medicare "open enrollment" period, which means you can choose any Medicare carrier without medical questions.

You only have ONE open enrollment period.

Make an informative choice during your open enrollment and possibly save hundreds of dollars each year! For more information on the choices and benefits available, return this postage paid inquiry card today!

( )YES! Also send me information on prescription discounts

Name_____          Sample OE1
Date of Birth_____
Spouse_____          John Q. Sample
Date of Birth_____          123 Main St.
Phone _____          City, ST 12345

PLEASE VERIFY ADDRESS AND PHONE # NOT AFFILIATED WITH OR ENDORSED BY ANY GOVERNMENT AGENCY

Type of Piece:   **"Take One" Leads**

Description:   This is self-generated; it is a mail-back piece that a salesperson places in a "Take One" dispenser in a high volume traffic area (e.g., grocery store, pharmacy, etc.)

When Received:  People drop the reply card in the mail; the salesperson receives it in two or three days.

Why Generated:  The people who see the display find something that may apply to them.

How Do You Approach:  The person you are approaching has taken the time to return the reply card and feels they may have an interest in one or more products.

When Do You Work the Lead:  These should be worked as soon as possible. It is very disturbing to the prospect when a salesperson does not respond promptly, after the prospect has put forth the effort to mail the reply card.

Product:   The display piece refers to a particular product. You should begin with this product, but it is only the door opener. By doing a proper job of fact-finding, you may discover other needs.

What Do You Say:  "Mrs. Jones, I am calling because you returned one of our mailers concerning (Product.) I may be able to help by reviewing your coverage and answering any questions you may have. I will be in your area on (Date). Would (3:00 or 4:00) be better for you?"

Type of Piece:    **Birthday Letter Leads**

Description:    This is self-generated; it results from a letter you mail to prospects who are turning 65. You follow up after sending the letter with a telephone call to set the appointment.

When Received:    The birthday letters should be done three to six months prior to the prospect's 65th birthday; they can be produced in conjunction with the "Turning 65" cards that are shipped to agency managers every six months.

Why Generated:    Ninety-five percent of all prospects buy a Medicare supplement policy within six months of their 65th birthday, because of Medicare's open enrollment during this time.

How Do You Approach:    These are people who are turning 65 years old. Your follow-up telephone calls should reference the birthday letter you recently mailed to them.

When Do You Work the Lead:    Any time the prospect is with six months of their 65th birthday, up to the month they actually turn 65. Medicare supplement policies may be written up to six months prior to the applicant's birthday, with coverage not starting until they go on Medicare (the first day of the month they turn 65.) PLEASE NOTE: People who turn 65 on the first day of the month start on Medicare the first day of the previous month.

Product:    Medicare supplement is usually the product. However, these people may be retiring and may lose their life insurance benefits from their employer. Also, they may need an annuity to roll over their retirement benefits from work. They may also need an immediate annuity to create an income stream. Long-Term Care insurance is another possibility. Many salespeople go for the Medicare supplement and fail to recognize and respond to the other insurance needs of the prospect. If we don't meet their needs, the competition WILL!

Don't forget, these people are accustomed to paying a considerable amount for their health care, even if they had coverage through their employer. This means that after retirement, after satisfying multiple needs, they may be paying less money than they had been before retirement.

What Do You Say:    "Mrs. Jones, I see you are turning 65 in (month.) I sent you a letter a few days ago Medicare supplement plans. Like most people, you probably have questions about Medicare. I will be in your area on (Date). Would (3:00 or 4:00) be better for you?"

**Type of Piece:**   Seminar Leads

**Description:**   This is self-generated; it results from an informational seminar you have presented on a particular subject to a group. Seminar presentation materials are available from your agency manager. The best seminars offer a free lunch or dinner after the presentation. You will set appointments individually while the prospects are eating.

**When Received:** The entire intent of a seminar is to generate a high-quality prospect. Seminars are for PROSPECTING, <u>not</u> SELLING.

**Why Generated:** These prospects have taken the time to attend the seminar because they are looking for information about a need they have.

**How Do You Approach:** The person you are approaching has already expressed an interest by attending your seminar. You need to set the appointments at the conclusion of the seminar, not with a follow-up telephone call.

**When Do You Work the Lead:** These prospects are eager to take care of their needs identified at the seminar. It is critical that you set the appointments as quickly as possible. People lose interest very easily. You should see the prospects within three days of the seminar.

**Product:**   The seminar lead is intended as a fact-finding mission. You should first introduce the product or concept the prospect has expressed interest in. The review may uncover other needs. By asking about the prospect's needs relating to other products, you may get additional sales. (For example, you may create an interest in Long-Term Care insurance by asking what the prospect has done to protect themselves from financial disaster resulting from a stay in a nursing home.)

**What Do You Say:** You say nothing! You set this appointment at the seminar!

## SEMINAR BASICS

Seminars can be an ideal marketing tool. Seminars enable you to immediately establish an environment where you may be perceived as a professional, creditable in your knowledge of the subject matter being presented. While you stand at the front of the room, you demonstrate that you have the experience necessary to provide trusted solutions to this new group of prospective clients. As you skillfully break down complicated issues to make them understandable, you prove yourself to be an expert worthy of the attendee's trust and eventually their business.

At the end of the seminar, attendees who entered the room strangers leave feeling assured they can entrust you with their confidence-and their business.

To ensure a seminar you hold doesn't' ruin your reputation or your finances the following is for seminars or workshops where you are also marketing your product or service in partnership with a client company or you have invited potential client companies.

## PLANNING

You must be organized. You must be thorough. And you must be creative. And most of all, you must be all these things before, during, and after your seminar.

## PREPARATIONS

When planning your business seminar, focus your efforts on three questions:
- *Who is my target audience?*
- *Which of their concerns could I effectively solve?*
- *What products would I actually use to solve their problems?*

> Prospective clients you invite to the seminar should be people that you feel could best benefit from the solutions you have to offer.

Prospective seminar attendees should include a mix of current clients/referrals and total strangers. Obviously, you will be much more successful at soliciting current customers to attend.

However, by blending current and prospective clients in the seminar room, you allow your present customers' positive comments to help build the confidence level of prospects that have never benefited from your services.

Current customers can also be a valuable source of additional prospects, since they may ask interested friends to join them at the seminar. Over time, this can provide you a pool of pre-qualified prospects you might otherwise have overlooked.

Once you have carefully determined your target audience, you are ready to plan the specifics of the seminar.

## SCHEDULE AND LOCATION

You should allow about six weeks between the day you determine your audience and the date your seminar will be held. The following format may be useful.

> Don't schedule your seminar immediately before or after a holiday. It will cut into your attendance and make follow-up appointments difficult to schedule.

An important step in planning your seminar is determining its location. Select a venue that is centrally located for your audience. Hopefully, your site will have convenient access and plenty of free parking. To locate your meeting room (and confirm its availability) call an appropriate hotel, restaurant, country club, or other civic building.

You should also predetermine the length of your seminar. The presentation itself will take about an hour. Allow time for mixing after engaging in questions and answers.

## CHECKLIST-THE DAY BEORE
Here is a suggested list:

For your guest:
*All seminar materials*
*Name tags*
*Sharpie pens (for attendees' use filling out name tags)*
*Supply of pencils*
*Refreshments/glasses*
*Attendee gifts (if applicable)*
*Supply of business cards*

For the presentation:
*List of confirmed attendees*
*Directional signs for site*
*Laptop computer/T.V./DVD*
*Video projector (if applicable)*
*Screen (if applicable)*
*Pointer*
*Remote control for projector (if applicable)*
*Stand for projector*
*Microphone/amplifier (if applicable)*
*Extension cords/power strips/three prong adapter*

# PREPARING SEMINAR MATERIALS

Once you have secured a convenient location for your seminar, take a moment to visualize how the seminar will actually come off:

**You as the attendee:**
- What will give you your first impression of the seminar?
- What path will you take to the seminar room?
- Will you receive clear direction to the room from professionally printed signs?
- Where will you hang your coat?
- Are there name tags? Do guest fill them out or does the presenter? Are the name tags on a table at the doorway-or inside the room?
- How will you be greeted?
- What will be on the table in front of you when you sit down at your place? Will there be a professionally printed seminar workbook, a pencil, a glass of water or other beverage?
  **Try to think of every detail, and jot down notes.**

Now turn to the tables and imagine yourself as presenter:

- Are you standing behind a podium?
- Is there a screen behind you? Is it directly behind you or to the side? Is the material on the screen easy to read?
- Does the room have to be darkened for maximum legibility? How do you turn off the lights or darken the windows?
- Do you have a pointer?
- Is there a microphone stand or clip-on mike? Where is the amplifier and sound control for it?
- What materials are at your fingertips?
- Are they on a table or stand? Can you reach them quickly and smoothly?

> Try to think of everything you will need to make your guests comfortable and then effectively present the seminar material. Then think of everything that could go wrong and, wherever possible, plan to provide a backup.

## CONFIRMING ATTENDANCE

After the mailing, if possible, handle all incoming phone confirmations personally. Take the opportunity to warmly thank callers for taking time out of their day to attend your seminar. Suggest that they are free to bring a friend. Make sure they know the easiest way to get to your seminar site form their home (of course you already know this, because you checked out the locations well in advance). And ask if they have any suggestions on a possible topic you should cover at the seminar.

> Send each phone confirmation a brief follow-up by mail or email. Type up a short master letter or email on company stationery, be sure to confirm the reservation and reiterate the seminar location, and highway access options.

Close this letter with the statement that you are anxious to see the attendee, and confident he or she will find the seminar's information valuable.

Call each mail respondent the day after you receive his or her response card. The purpose of this call is to cover the same points outlined immediately above.

Call every respondent a second time, approximately three days before the seminar. Briefly remind them of the seminar. Briefly remind them of the time and date, and tell them you're looking forward to seeing them. Make absolutely certain they know how to find the seminar site by relating it to a landmark or intersection.

Finally, on the day immediately preceding your seminar, check your appearance.

- Will you be wearing a neatly pressed conservative business attire, to enhance the audience's perception that you are an experienced professional
- Is you hair neatly trimmed? Are accessories like you tie shoes, etc. ready to reinforce your image and build credibility?

Your seminar is essentially a job interview.

You're asking every member of your audience to trust you and hire you.

Look the part.

## THE SEMINAR

Most successful seminars actually begin the evening before their schedule start time. This is the time for you to carefully go over you Six Week Checklist and make sure every item has been addressed. It's also a good time to take a quiet moment to walk through your seminar in your mind. Go back and imagine you are one of your seminar guests, just as we described in the earlier section.

This time, however, your visualization of the seminar should be decidedly different from your previous walk through. This time, every detail you visualize should be accounted for and in place. If you think of any loose ends (or any nice touches), resolve them before the day of the seminar. Be certain to note any loose ends on a final checklist. It will be a valuable resource for future seminars you give.

Another important item to address the day before the seminar is how you will open and close your presentation. Tailor your remarks to the specific audience you'll be addressing. If you will be relying on an icebreaker or humorous anecdote to get the seminar started, nail it down now. If you need to "borrow" an icebreaker, watch the late night talk shows with pen and remote control in hand. Flip back and forth until you catch a topical humorous remark you feel comfortable incorporating into the following day's presentation. Write the icebreaker down word for word. Then get a good night's sleep.

If you have any appointments on the day of your seminar, make certain they can be wrapped up well before the seminar begins. You should make sure you can get to the seminar site at least an hour before your scheduled start time.

Before you leave for the seminar, do two things. First, take another look at your final checklist and be sure everything you need is either at the site or in your trunk. Second, make sure an associate is available to field any last minute calls from attendees. Leave behind your cell phone number and a map showing the site highlighted with the routes you suggested attendees take to get to it.

If possible, have a second associate come to the seminar site with you. This person can help greet guest as they arrive, and can serve as back-up to help everything go smoothly during your presentation. When you arrive at the seminar site, be sure everything in the room is set up at least 30 minutes in advance.

If you are using directional signs, make sure they are in place. Check the microphone, sound levels, room lighting and projector. Slowly walk around the room to see if there are any seats that are undesirable because of glare. Arriving early will also give you a chance to relax-and to warmly greet any guests who arrive early, which they will.

# THE PRESENTATION

Here are some suggestions to help assure your presentation goes off without a hitch.

## BE CORDIAL

Many of your guests may come to your seminar fearful they'll be a captive audience for a 60-minute sales pitch. Put their fears to rest. Today, you're in the information business. Your mission is to demonstrate your ability to solve their problems, period.

## WARM UP THE ROOM

About 10 minutes before your presentation's scheduled start time, begin a conscious effort to nurture a warm, friendly environment. Casually ask you attendees one-on-one about their families, etc. Check to see everyone has all the materials they will need for the next hour (of course they do-you double checked everything well before they arrived).

## HAVE YOUR ASSOCIATE TAKE ATTENDANCE

You'll want a record of who attended your seminar. Go around the room asking each attendee to state his name and city. The attendees can record their names on a questionnaire. You can collect them at the end of the seminar.

## START ON TIME. END ON TIME.

Get the ball rolling by referring to the diversity of your audience's. Contrast that with their common problems-the ones you will be addressing in your presentation. State unequivocally that your goal will be to show how other individual's have confronted and resolved these problems with your professional guidance. Tell your audience you are hoping they will similarly rely upon you as future clients. Then launch into your presentation.

## REFER TO YOU HANDOUT MATERIALS

Hopefully, you've selected your support materials because they emphasize and expand the points you will be driving home in you presentation. Be sure to mention them during your presentation so your audience realizes how valuable they are.

## STATE YOUR CONCLUSION UNEQUIVOCALLY

Your goal has been to identify general problems and concerns shared by the attendees. In your presentation, you've given actionable solutions to those common concerns. Remind your audience that their individual problems and concerns are unique. You are confident you have demonstrated that you can be counted on for creative solutions to your audience's individual challenges.

## ASK FOR THE CONFIDENCE AND RESPONSE OF YOUR AUDIENCE

Among the materials given to your guests was a questionnaire. At the end of the seminar, ask your guests to please take a moment fill it out. Ask them to fill out the request for additional information. Let your guest know you will review all the questionnaires immediately after the seminar, and promise to call each participant within 48 hours.

## DON'T ASK, "DOES ANYONE HAVE ANY QUESITONS?

More often than not, those five words will bring the momentum you've built to a screeching halt. The time for individual questions will occur as you mingle after the seminar.

## CLOSE THE SEMINAR BY "LEAVING THE DOOR OPEN"

When you reach the schedule ending time for your seminar, stop to note the time and warmly thank your guests. Hopefully, you will have received a cue from your associate to let you know your scheduled time is ending (this will allow you to keep focused on your guests, not your watch). Cordially let your guests know they can remain to ask questions or call you tomorrow. Then immediately move to a position from which you can shake each attendee's hand and thank them as they leave the seminar room. If you promised each guest a gift, hand it to them individually.

## BEFORE YOU HIT THE ROAD, JOT DOWN YOUR THOUGHTS

When the last guest has left, immediately grab a legal pad or hand held tape recorder. Stand at the podium and imagine the room as it had been a few minutes earlier. Recall the faces and names of your guests, and jot down or record anything you can remember about them, including specific concerns they might have voiced. Don't leave the room until you've done this.

## FOLLOW UP

As we have discussed your seminar presentation, we cautioned you that at your seminar you were in the information business. That remains true when you make follow-up calls to your seminar guests.

## SET THE APPOINTMENTS YOURSELF

During your seminar, you worked hard to establish a relationship with your guests. Maintain that feeling of trust by calling them personally to set their appointment times. The information you need is on the questionnaire they completed and you collected at the close of your seminar. Be sure to make all appointments follow-up calls within the time frame promised at your seminar, usually 48 hours.

## SEND A LETTER OR EMAIL TO CONFIRM THE DETAILS

The day after you set up an appointment time over the phone, send each client a brief written confirmation. This letter or email can mirror the one you sent to confirm their attendance at your seminar. Mention the date/time/location of the meeting, and close by mentioning you are looking forward to the meeting.

## THE COMPLEMENTARY CONSULTATION

Here is a brief synopsis of the client meetings you'll host as a result of your seminar. Obviously, you will create a meeting agenda that suits your presentation skills and your client's temperament. A typical meeting might go something like this:

:00-05-The meeting begins on time, starting with a very loose agenda

:05-35-Spend about half an hour listening. Review the information the client furnished on the questionnaire. Let the client fully explain the specific concerns or questions they have.

: 35-55-Over the next 20 minutes, review the solutions you have available. Don't overwhelm the client with product specifics or dazzle him or her with charts and illustrations. Rather, suggest that the client's concerns are very "solvable," and that you can likely think of a number of ways to resolve them. Cite specifics as part of a framework of general ways you can serve his or her "big picture" strategy. This way, if a client balks at a specific recommendation, you'll be able to retreat and regroup with another plan.

: 55-60-If you feel comfortable, do a trial close. Otherwise, conclude the meeting by promising to get in touch with hard numbers and concrete suggestions within the next 48 hours. This will give clients the breathing room they may need to accept your consider your plan, then wholeheartedly accept your suggestions.

This seminar outline is only a suggestion. It is important to research this information as it relates to you specific area.

Good luck and good selling.

# Seminar Guide – DO'S AND DON'TS

| SEMINARS<br>You want attendees who want the following: | DO's<br>Things you want to do | DON'T<br>Things you don't' want |
|---|---|---|
| Average Attendance | 25-50 | 0 to 10 |
| Earnings per Attendee | $500 - $1,000 | 0 to $100 |
| Earnings per Seminar | $12,000 to $20,000 | 0 to $1,000 |
| Cost per Seminar (Mail & lunch) | $250 to $1,000 | No refreshments |
| Sponsoring partners | Wants an extra $25,000 $50,000 in commissions'<br>Has client base<br>Strong, positive relationship With clients<br>Can close, but has no clients<br>Combination of closer with Client base agent | Any non-producing partner<br>Happy with extra $100<br>Never sees clients<br>Doesn't follow up |
| Client Attendees | Best client prospects in order<br>CEO/COO/CFO clients<br>Long-term clients<br>Corporate clients with budget<br>Prospects with stated issues | Any mail lists available<br>Recent customer<br>Any warm body |
| Seminar Invitation | Must include "How to" points Of interest<br>Should identify sponsoring partners and be signed<br>May include personal note Stating "Bring a friend"<br>Use quality paper | Design your own Just telephone and save on mailing and printing costs |

| SEMINARS | DO's | DON'T |
|---|---|---|
| Seminar Place | Easily accessible<br>Close to clients homes/business<br>Free parking<br>Perceived as "nice place"<br>Best choices with meals:<br>Hotels/Motels/Church social halls<br>Best choices without meals:<br>Retirement activity centers/Office conference rooms | Pick cheapest site<br>site regardless of<br>location |
| Seminar Time | Not too early<br>Not too late<br>Not during commuter rush hours<br>Only one seminar per day<br>Tuesday, Wednesday or Thursday<br>Best schedule:<br>9:30 coffee<br>10:00 seminar<br>11:15 lunch | Most convenient<br>for speaker not<br>clients<br>7:00 a.m.<br>8:00 p.m.<br>Schedule two or<br>three per day so<br>you can repeat<br>two or three times<br>for same overall<br>attendance<br>Serve just coffee |
| Seminar Size | Attendance varies by strength of<br>Speaker/client relationship:<br>500 to 1,000 invitations<br>35 to 60 "RSVPs"<br>25 to 50 attendees | Mail only 25 sure<br>suspects<br>Wait for them to<br>show an interest |

| SEMINARS | DO's | DON'Ts |
|---|---|---|

Seminar Preparation:

| | | |
|---|---|---|
| Minus 6 weeks | Watch Previous/other seminar<br>Select and confirm meeting site<br>Requirements | Just dream<br>about fees |
| Minus 4 weeks | Print enough sets for expected<br>Attendance plus 10 | |
| Minus 3 weeks | Separate by pages –50 page ones,<br>50 pages twos<br>Mail invitations first class | Ask vendor office<br>to print |
| Minus 2 weeks | Verify number of responses | vendor office |
| Minus 1 week | Call responders to remind/confirm<br>Call enough non-responders to fill<br>Room. "We are ordering lunches<br>For our client luncheon. Will you be<br>Able to attend, or would you prefer a<br>Private meeting to learn how to ......" | Cancel |
| Minus 1 day | Meet with site manager and review<br>Requirements<br>"U" shape with dining tables behind<br>tables alone<br>All tables placed so speaker can be heard<br>And seen without continual turning<br>Setting at tables organized facing speaker<br>Pencils and paper at each setting<br>Registration table at entrance<br>No podium-speaker should walk among<br>Clients<br>Small table upfront for speaker<br>Larger table at both sides of room to hold<br>Sets of pages<br>Easel up front listing sponsoring partners with<br>sponser names<br>Meeting notice in lobby<br>Parking validation procedures<br>All supplies at site, if shipped<br>Settings at tables comfortably spaced<br>Hot buffet or pre-selected lunch meal<br>Room clean<br>Heating/air conditioning temperatures moderate | Never coordinate with<br>site manager |

| SEMINARS | DO's | DON'Ts |
|---|---|---|
| Meet with partners | Review what will take place<br>Review sequence of events<br>Assign roles to sponsoring and observing partners<br>*ABOVE ALL*, instruct them to mix with clients<br>Not with other partners | Assume they know what to do |
| Meeting Day | | |
| Prior to meeting | Final review with site manager<br>Final review with partners<br>Check off attendees on registration list<br>Name tags with BIG first names only,<br>So speaker can involve audience<br>Make sure coffee/cold drinks are set up<br>*MIX* with early arrivals to show friendship<br>And real concern for their financial well being | Show up just prior to meeting<br>Show up with no name tags |
| During meeting | Pass out pages as speaker reads any pages<br>One partner per table speeds up meeting and<br>Keeps continuity of seminar flowing | Talk with other partners and not clients<br>Leave room to<br>Make telephone<br>Calls<br>Eat and talk with<br>Other partners not<br>Clients |
| During lunch | If not enough partners, sponsor should table<br>Hop and mix with each client during lunch<br>Talk about how products/services, give them<br>Choices. | Eat and talk with other agents not |

**Cost**

Get quotes on meals, coffee, drinks, easels, etc.
Underestimate attendance, you will always be
Glad to pay more if more show

Speaker Duties

Involve attendees, use first names
Kickoff-THANK YOU to your clients
Big buildup of sponsoring agency experience,
Expertise and reputation
Poll audience-What do clients think of when they
Think of Social Security, Medicare, Long Term Care?
Start by reading invitation promises
Now, agency will fulfill promises
Speak in general terms so everyone understands what is said
Free 30-minute interview will cover your actual situation
Door prize for completing first page-$50 cash for gourmet
Dinner for two works well (whatever you do have ready)
Follow seminar as learned
Add color stories or personal experiences _"my father"
"My grandmother"-that relate to subjects being discussed
Go slow and have them make notes to review with their agent
*LAST PAGE* is reviewed of "Free 30-minute confidential review"
Be sure to check items you want further information on
Fill out appointment preference
Name and telephone number for door prize
Draw winner
MIX with clients during lunch
See every attendee

# Epilogue

In this book we discussed what and how you need to develop a business plan, we exampled an income model and looked at the different lead types you can use to grow your business.

Handling objections was reviewed with several techniques explored and illustrated so you can better focus on the things that matter most to your prospects. It is important that you always sell the "problem" and "tell" the solution.

Various scripts were illustrated based on lead types, including what and how to handle each lead type, the approach you might use along some principles to be successful.

Included in the lead types was Seminar marketing and we broke down why you might consider seminars, how to schedule these seminars; manage the attendees and a step-by-step guide for actually conducting the seminar and the Do's and Don'ts for a successful seminar.

You have what it takes to grow your business, you are as smart as the most successful agent and your family deserves to live the lifestyle you secretly want to provide them.

You are the "**NEXT**" thing you do, so step out, make mistakes and do your "**NEXT**" big thing. Selling is a contact profession, remember the more you sweat in training the less you bleed in battle.

Continuously review your training material, including this book, continually attend training and practice, practice, practice, and make mistakes. Making mistakes won't kill you, it won't cause a life threating illness, however making mistakes will provide the lessons you can use to a 6 figure income a build a 7 figure business.

Get a great lead vendor, one that doesn't just sell you leads but one that helps you develop a strategy to get in front of the prospects who meeting your target market. These books was co-written by my friend Richard Bufkin with Target Leads, the best direct mail lead company in the business in my opinion, but use one who is willing to be accountable, who gives you feedback and is in it with you to grow your business.

Stay plugged in, join http://7figuresalestools.com/ and take advantage of the community of fellow sales professionals who are honing their skills, developing their selling style and increasing their income by growing their client base along with the wallet share they have in each home.

Let us know how we can help you grow………

Keep falling forward.

# PRINCIPLES FROM *"HOW TO WIN FRIENDS AND INFLUENCE PEOPLE."* (by

Dale Carnegie *1888-1955* founder of the Carnegie Course)

## *BECOME A FRIENDLIER PERSON:*

1. Don't criticize, condemn or complain.
2. Give honest, sincere appreciation.
3. Arouse in the other person an eager want.
4. Become genuinely interested in other people.
5. Smile.
6. Remember that a person's name is to that person the most important sound in any language.
7. Be a good listener. Encourage others to talk about themselves.
8. Talk in terms of the other person's interest.
9. Make the other person feel important - and do so sincerely.
10 The only way to get the best of an argument is to avoid it.

## *WIN PEOPLE TO YOUR WAY OF THINKING:*

11. Show respect for the other person's opinions. Never say, "You're wrong."
12. If you are wrong, admit it quickly and emphatically.
13. Begin in a friendly way.
14. Get the other person saying, "Yes, yes" immediately.
15. Let the other person do a great deal of the talking.
16. Let the other person feel that the idea is his or hers.
17. Try honestly to see things from the other person's point of view.
18. Be sympathetic with the other person's ideas and desires.
19. Appeal to the nobler motives.
20. Dramatize your ideas.

## *BE A LEADER:*

21. Throw down a challenge.
22. Begin with praise and honest appreciation.
23. Call attention to people's mistakes indirectly.
24. Talk about your own mistakes before criticizing the other person.
25. Ask questions instead of giving direct orders.
26. Let the other person save face.
27. Praise the slightest and every improvement. Be "lavish in your praise."
28. Give the other person a fine reputation to live up to.
29. Use encouragement. Make the fault seem easy to correct.
30. Make the other person happy about doing the thing you suggest.

CPSIA information can be obtained
at www.ICGtesting.com
Printed in the USA
BVHW020338211218
536164BV00010B/384/P

*  9 7 8 1 5 4 4 2 8 0 5 6 1  *